THE NARRATIVE

OF THE

PILGRIM'S PROGRESS

FROM

THIS WORLD TO THAT WHICH IS TO COME.

BY JOHN BUNYAN.

Printed in the Corresponding Style of Phonography.

LONDON:

F. PITMAN, PHONETIC DEPOT, 20 PATERNOSTER ROW, E.C.

BATH:

ISAAC PITMAN, PHONETIC INSTITUTE.

1876.

BATH : PRINTED BY ISAAC PITMAN,

PHONETIC INSTITUTE.

THE STORY OF
THE PILGRIM'S PROGRESS.

—:o:—

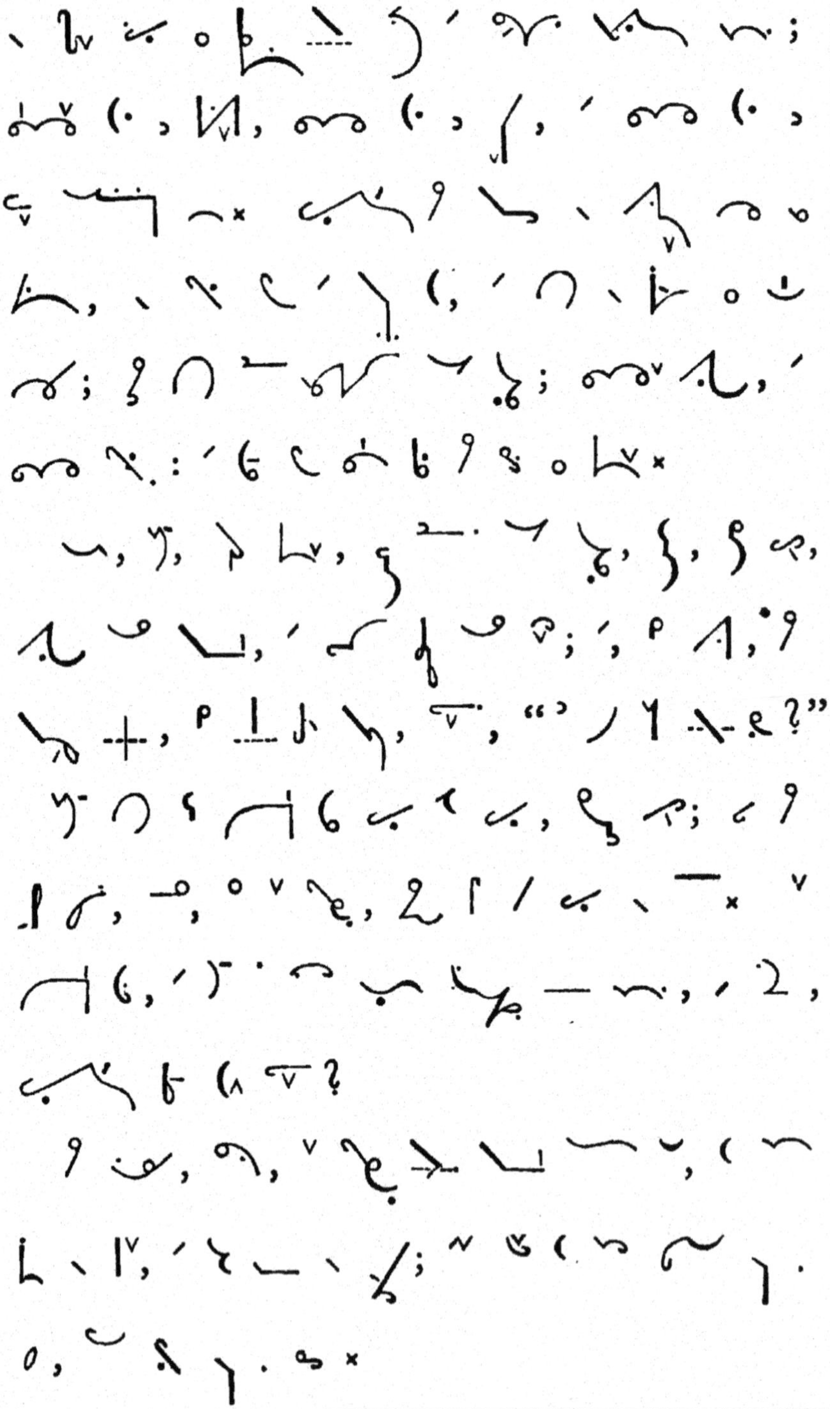

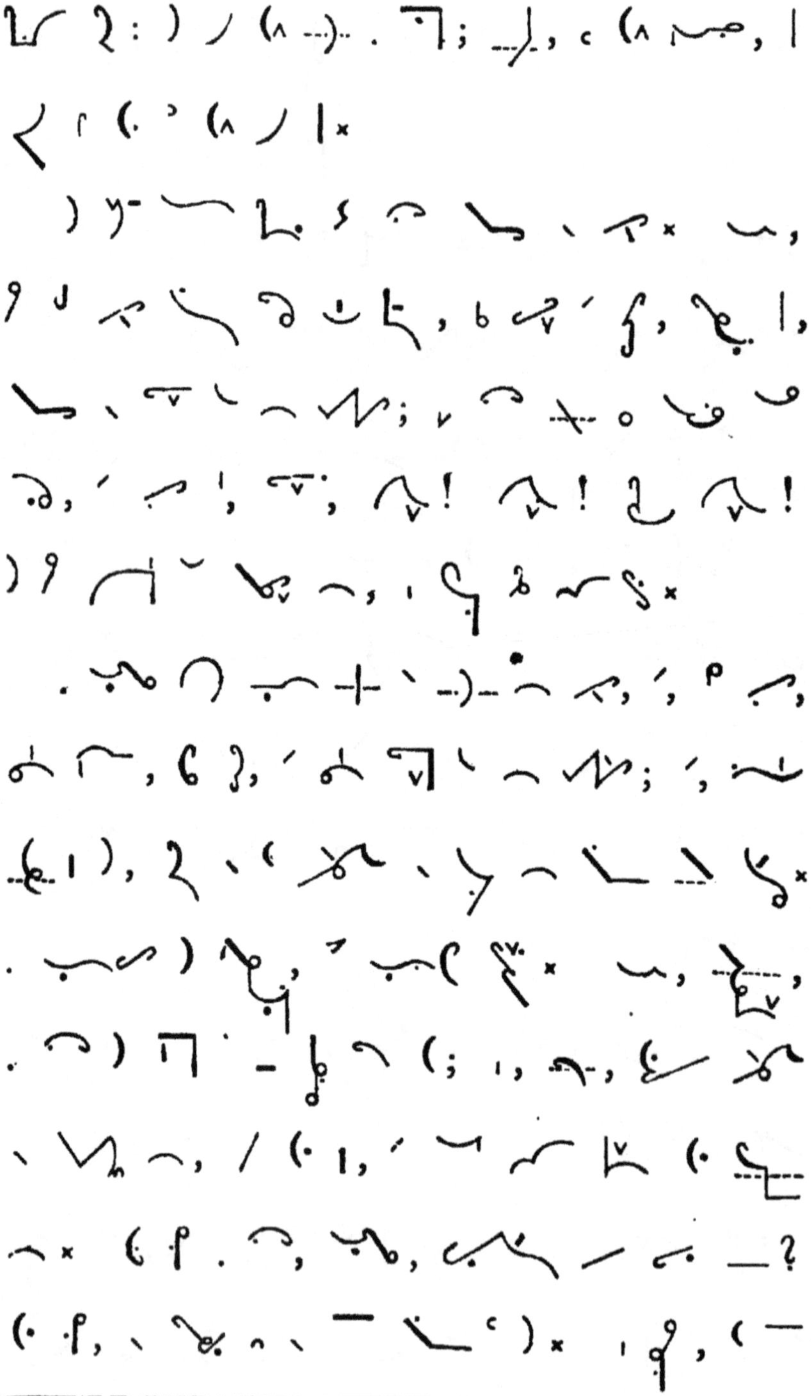

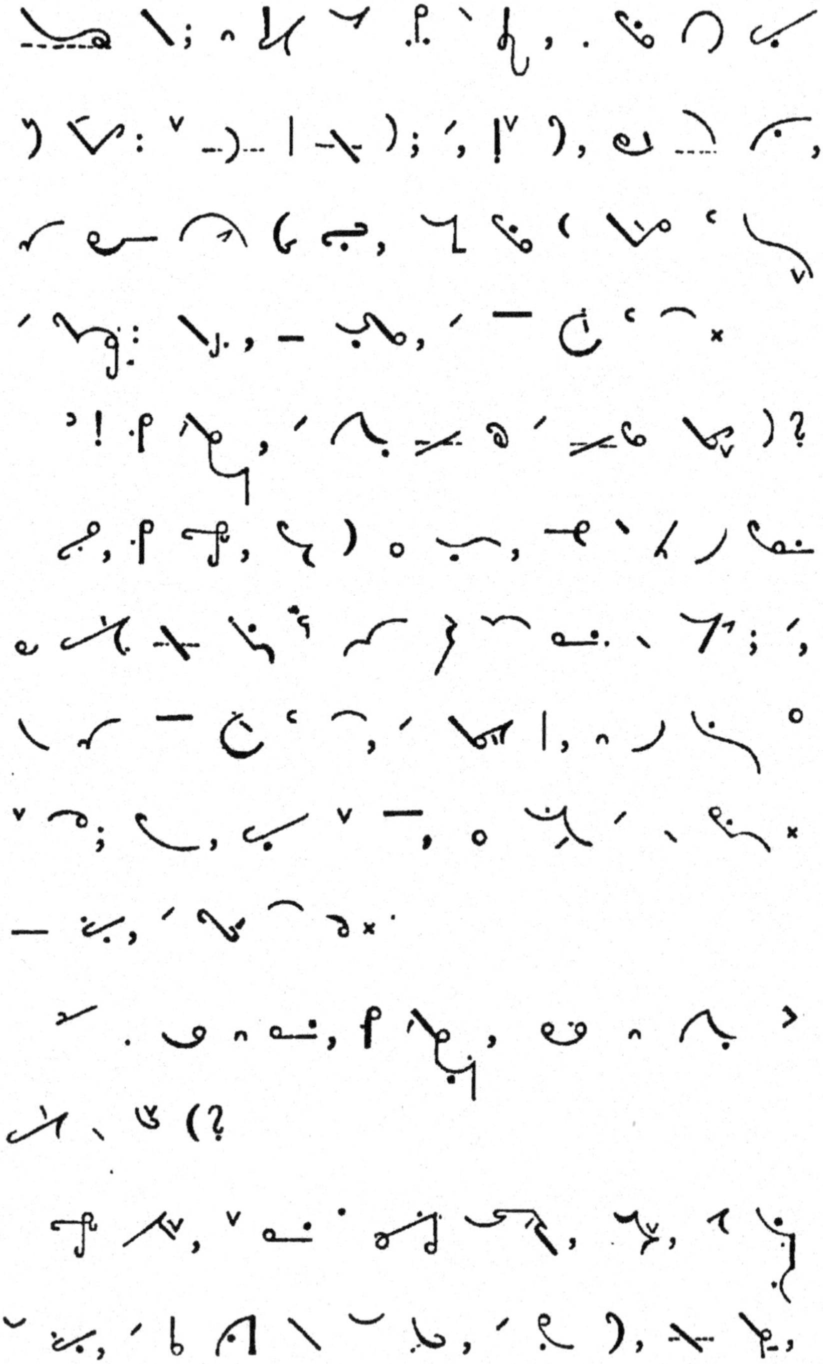

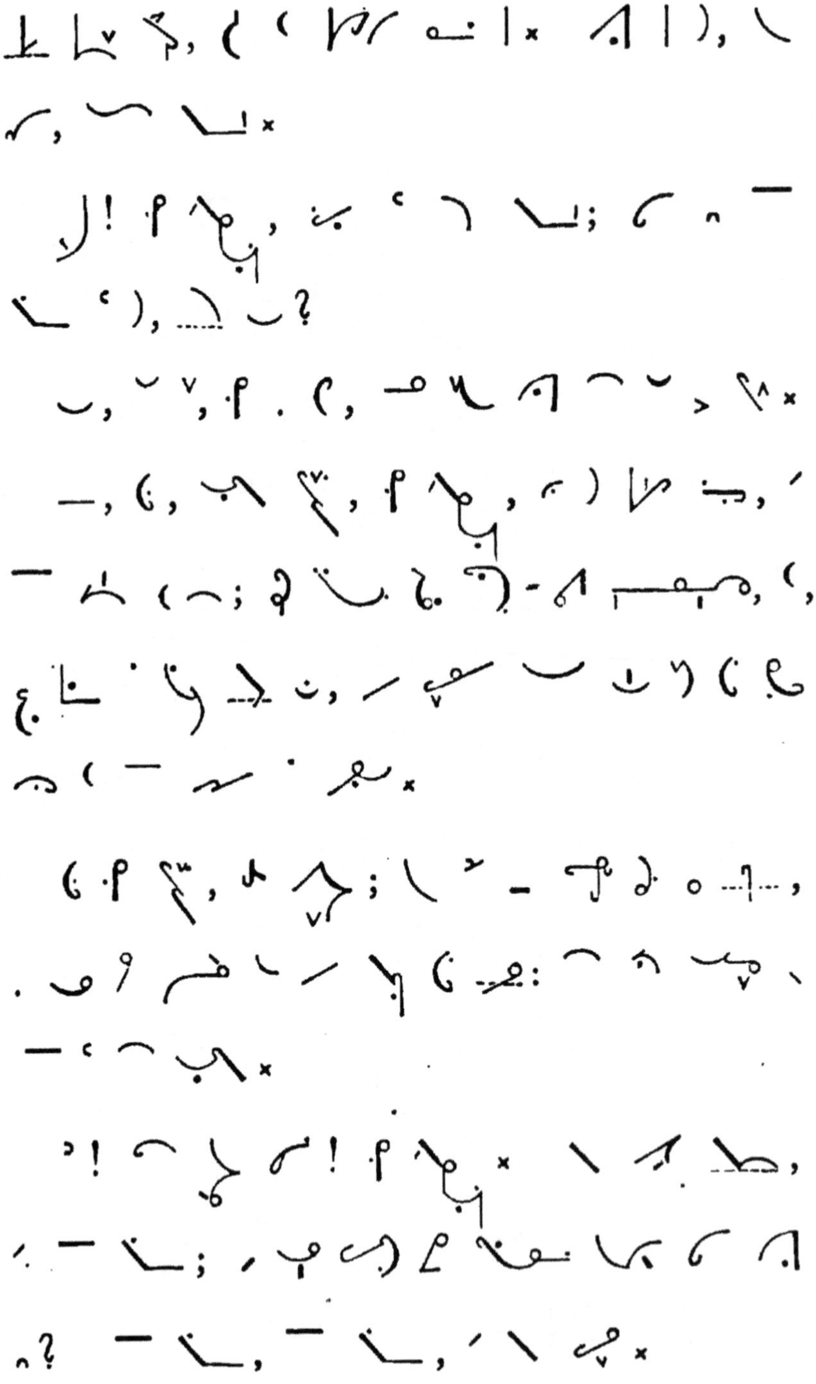

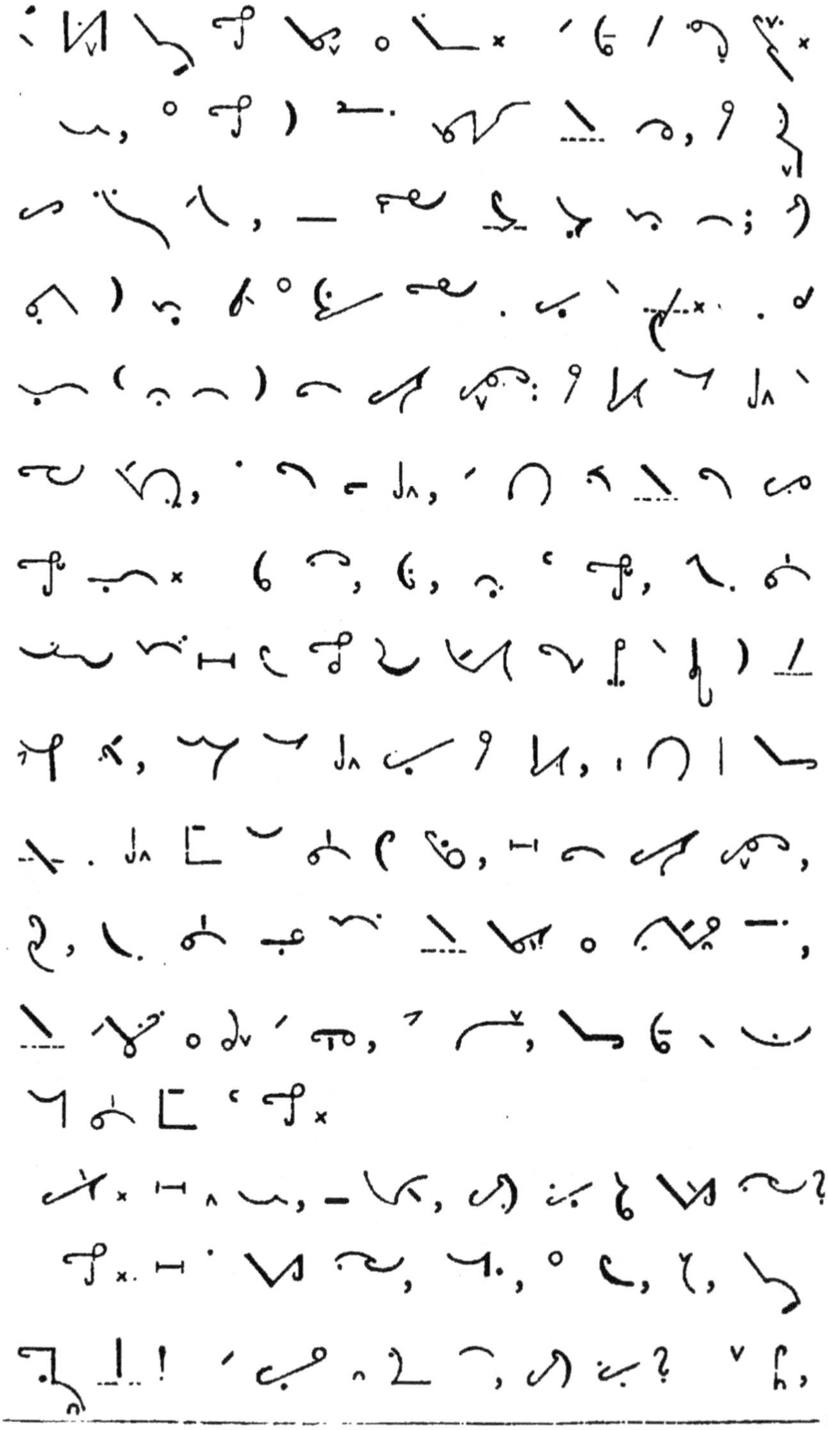

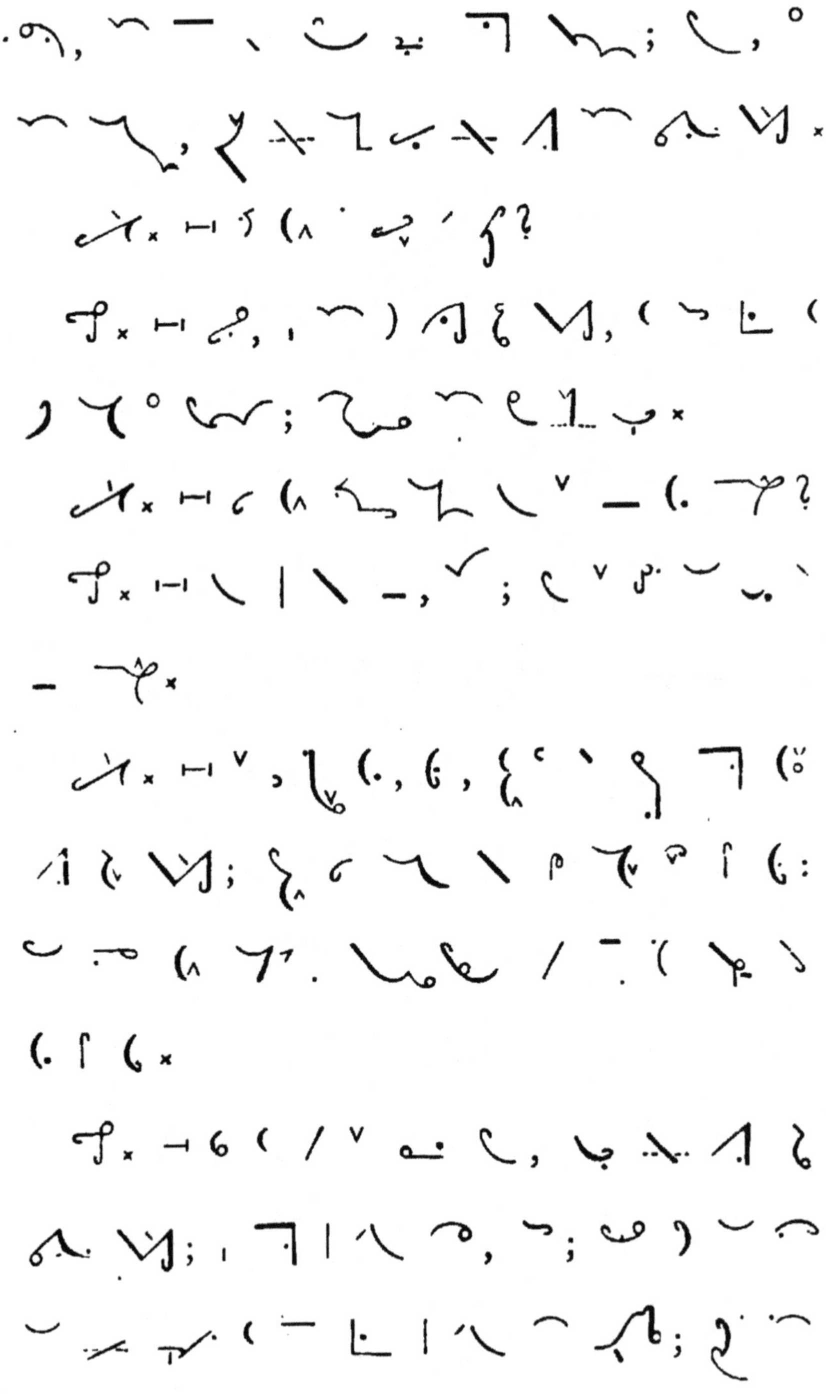

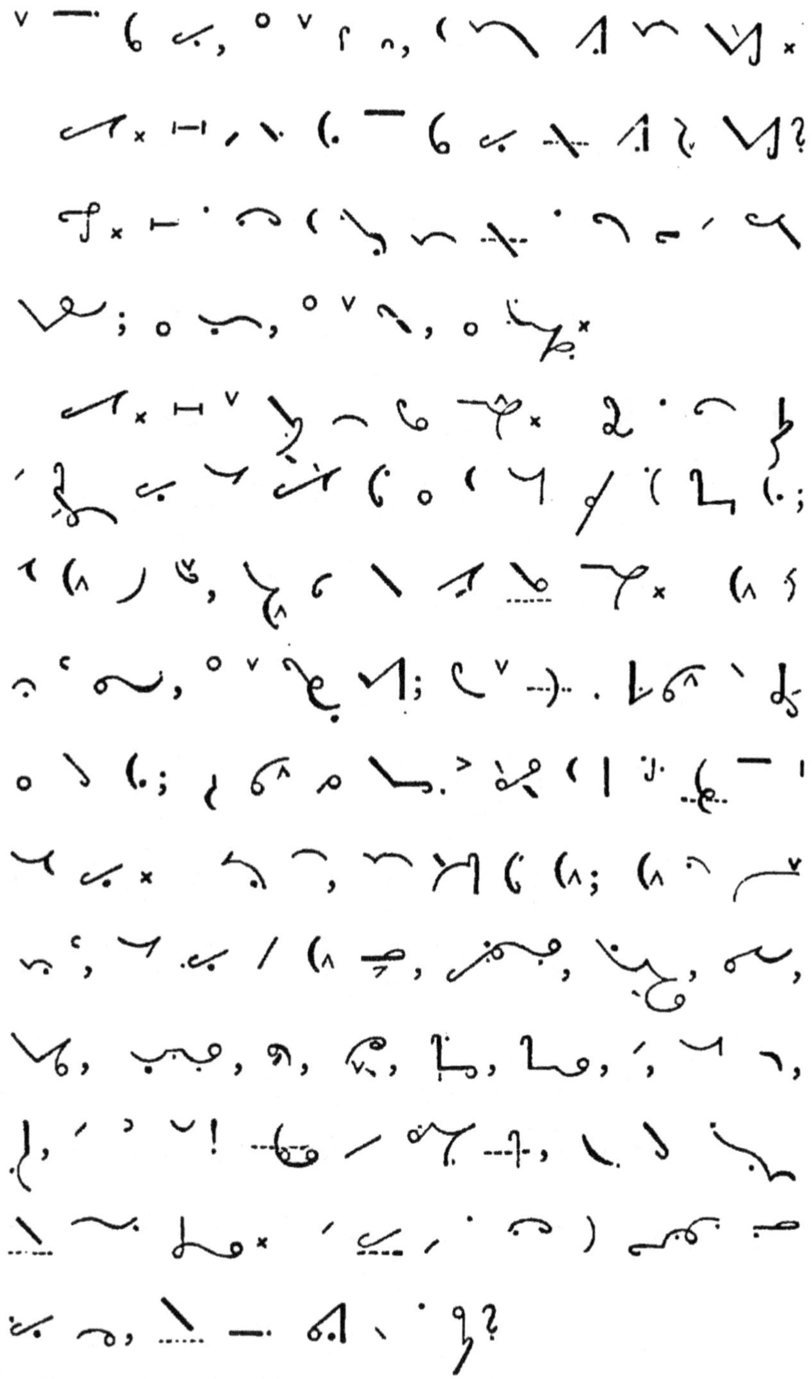

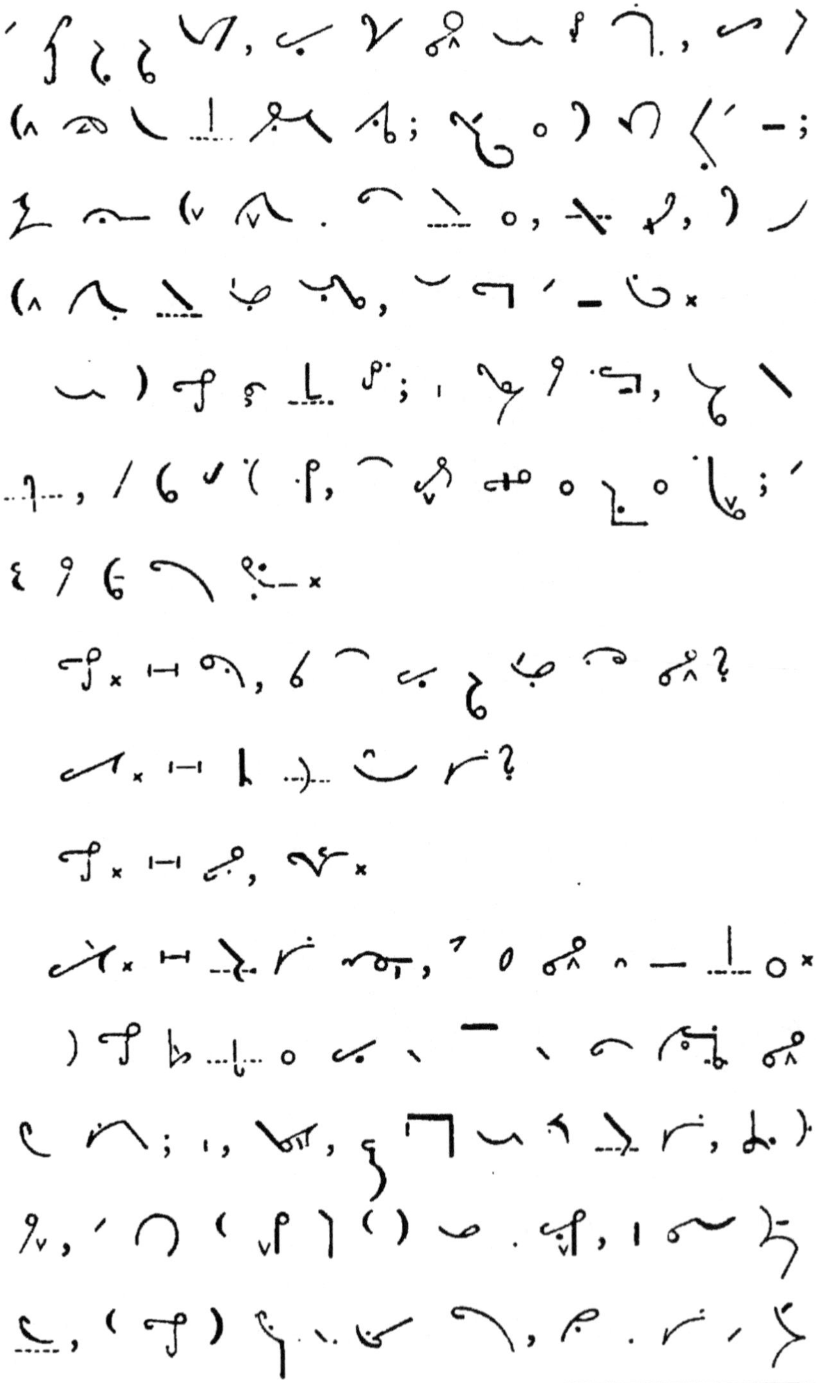

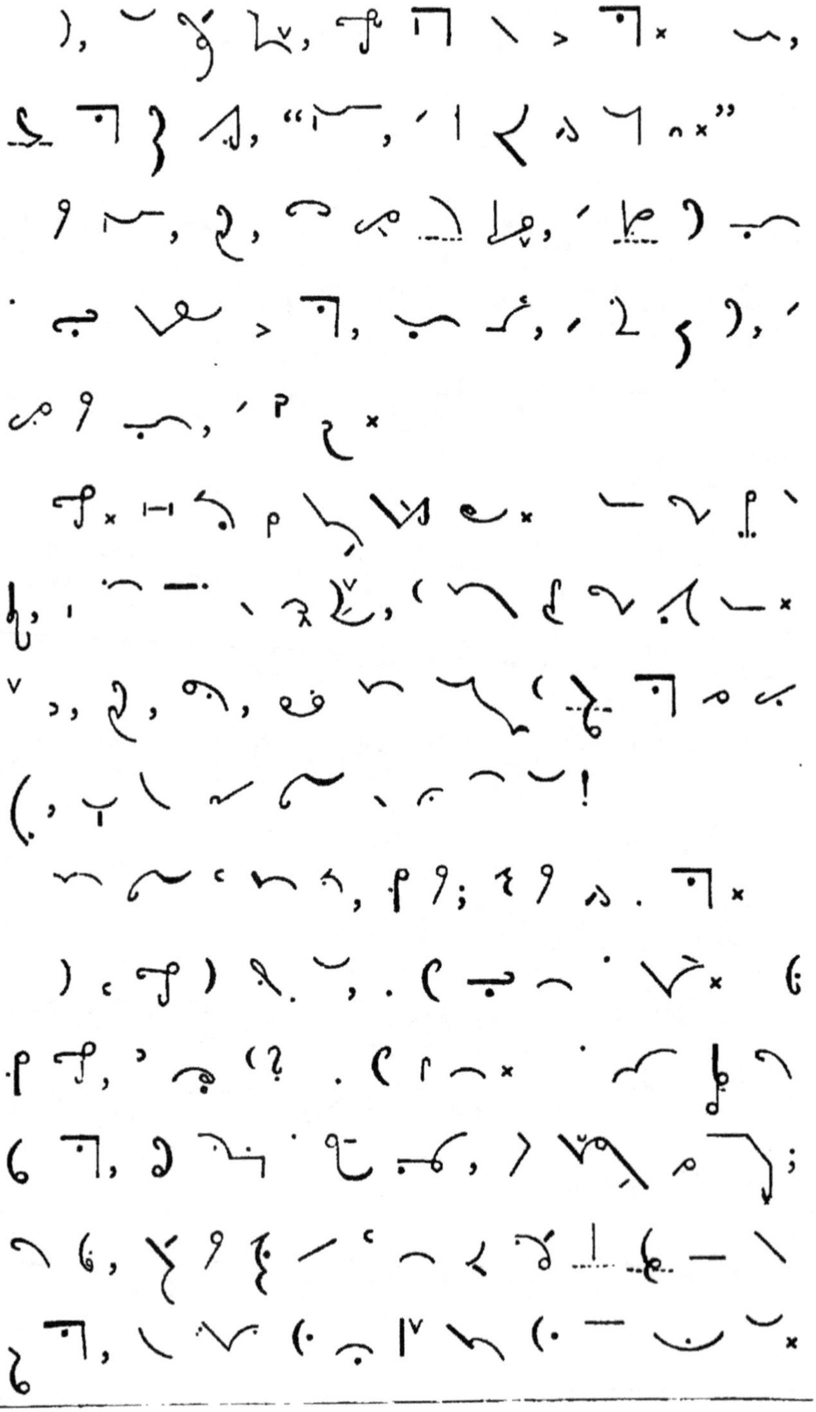

[Page of shorthand script — not transcribable as text]

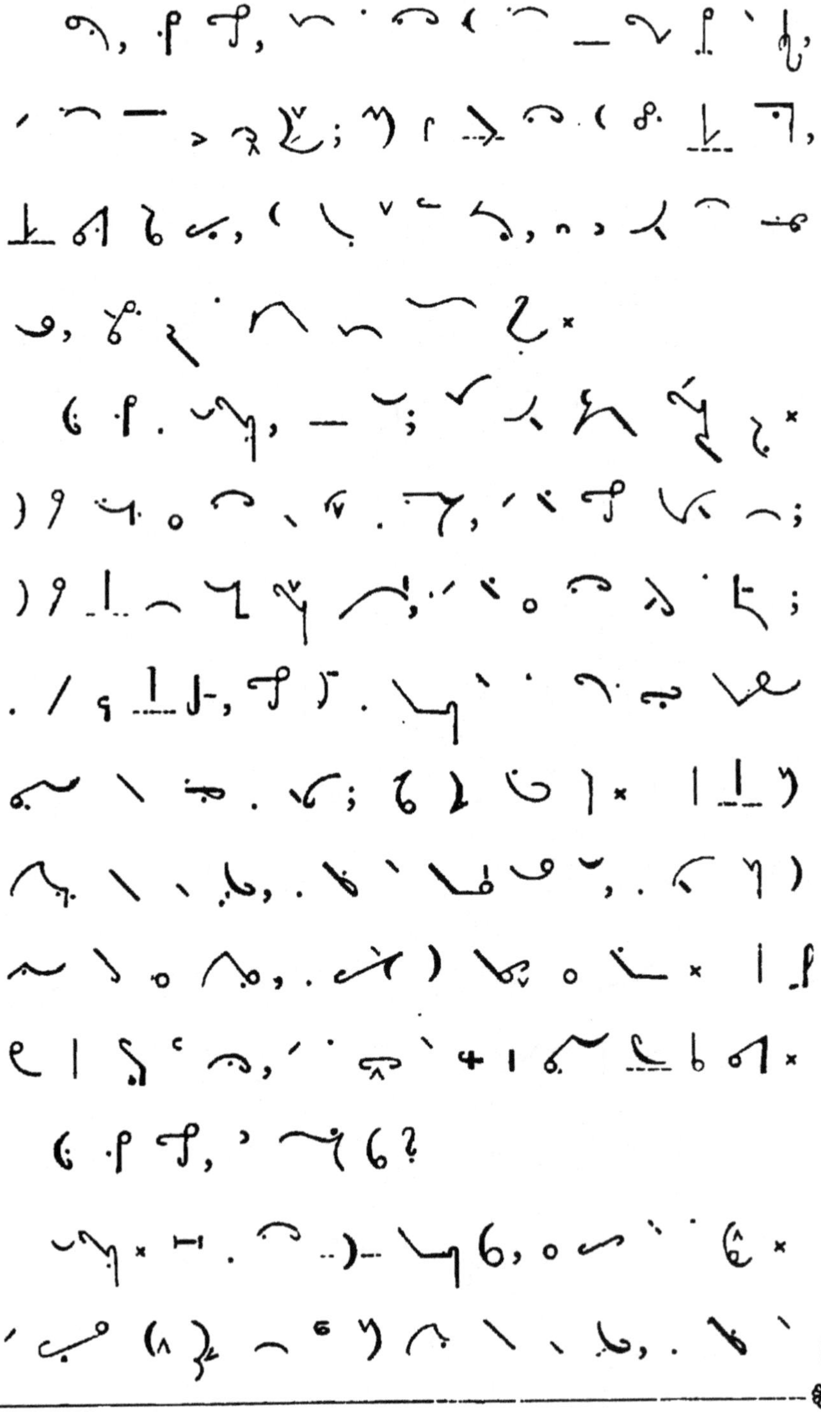

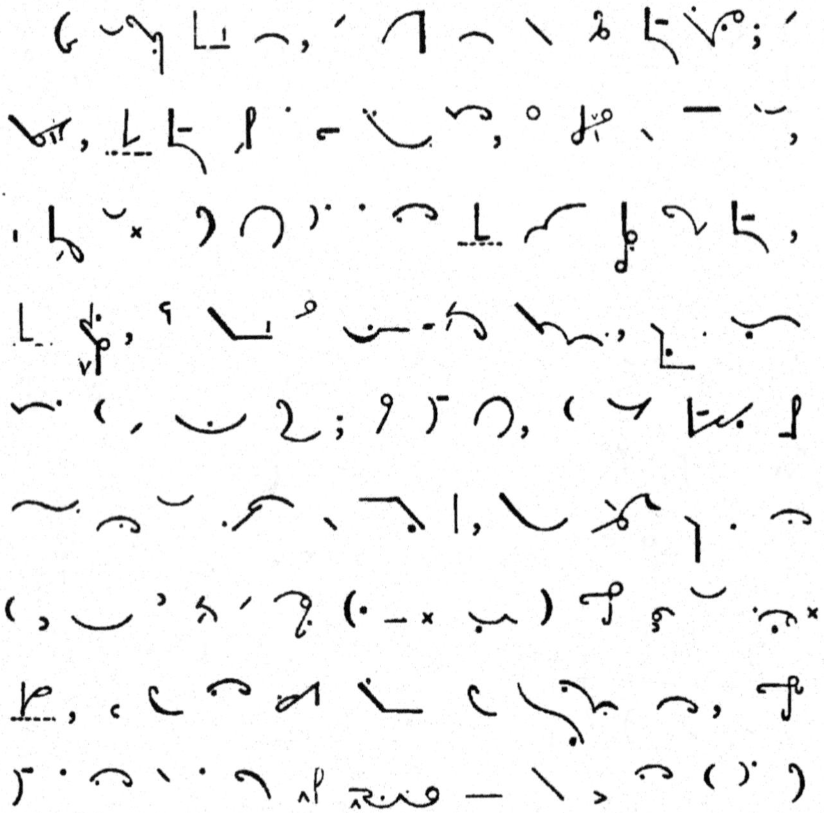

(shorthand text)

[Shorthand text - not transcribable as Latin characters]

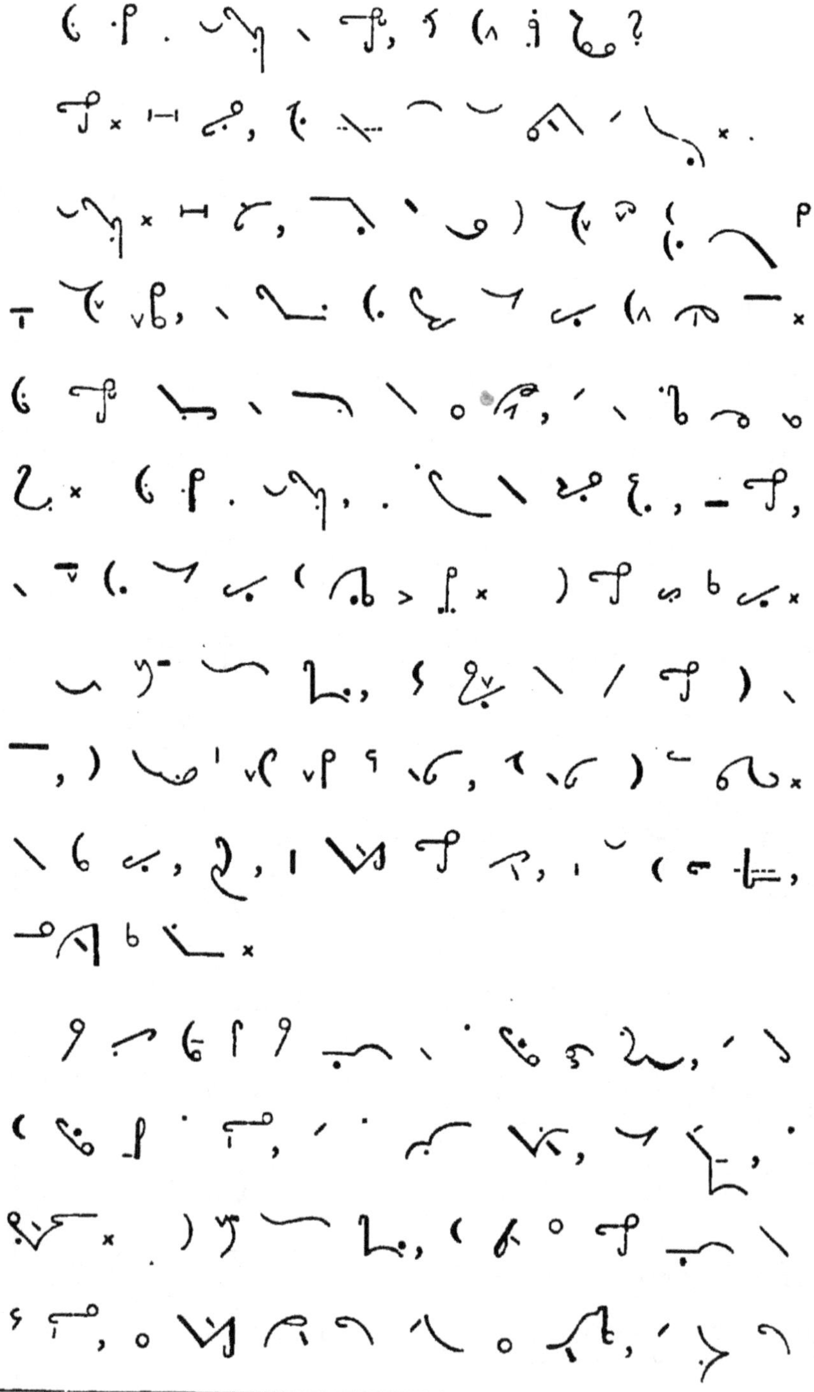

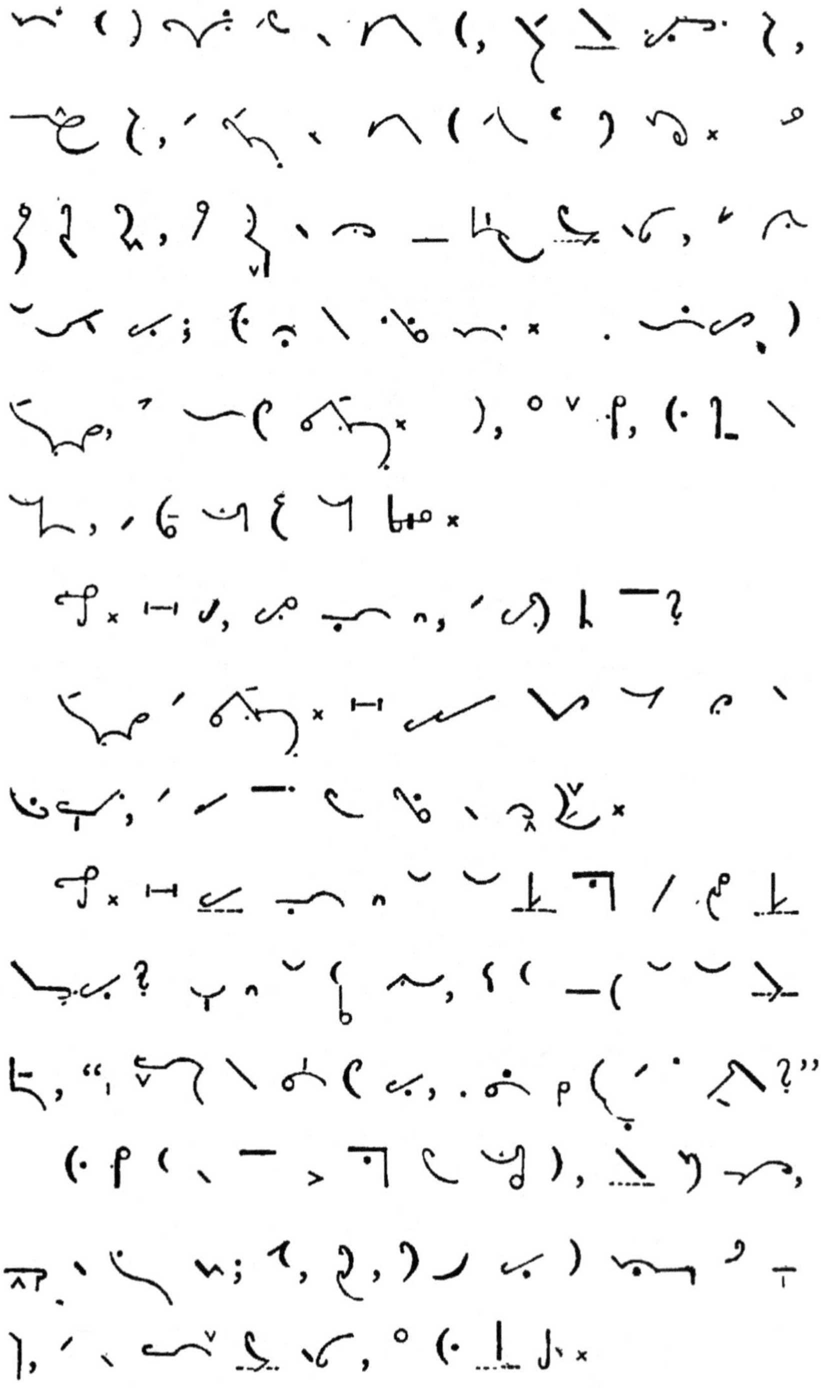

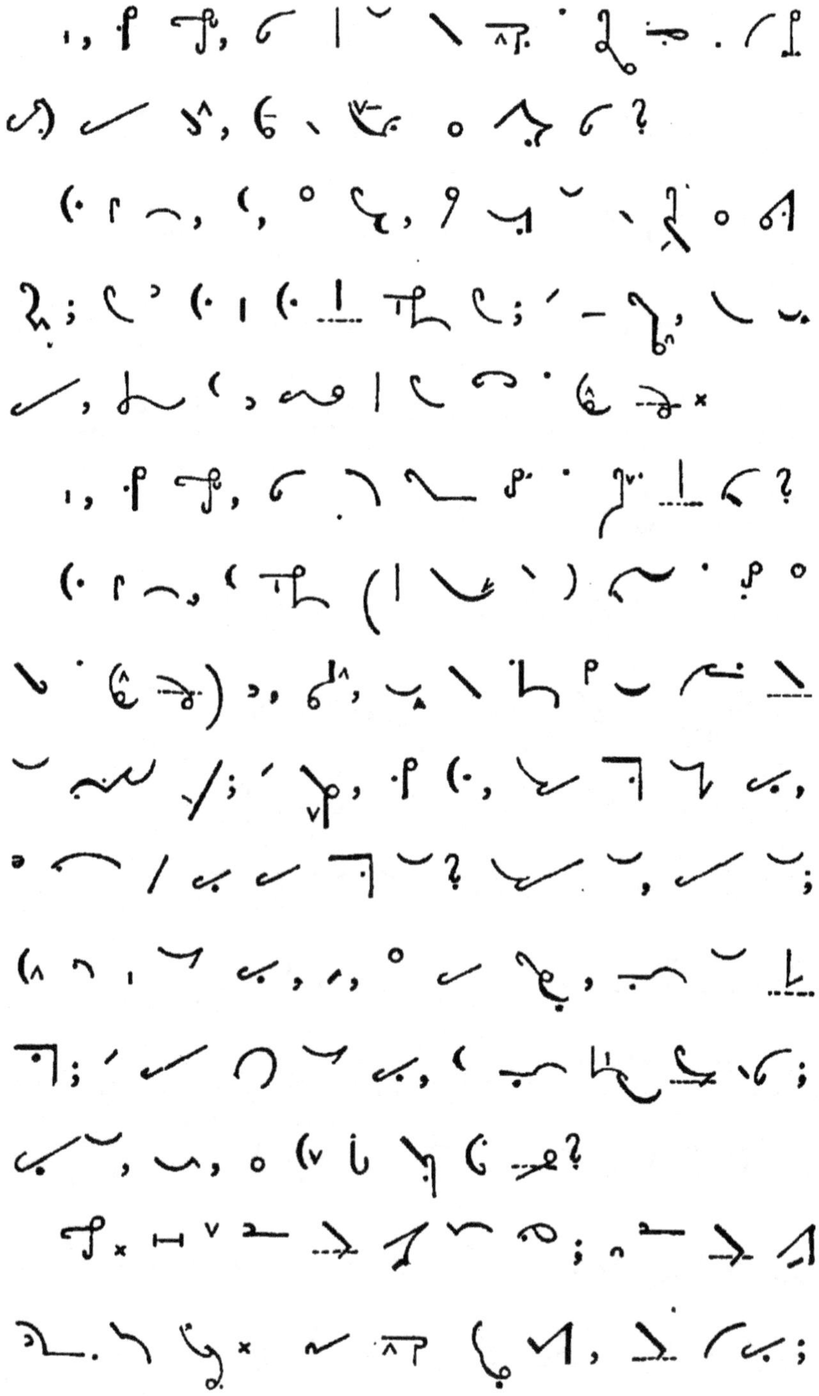

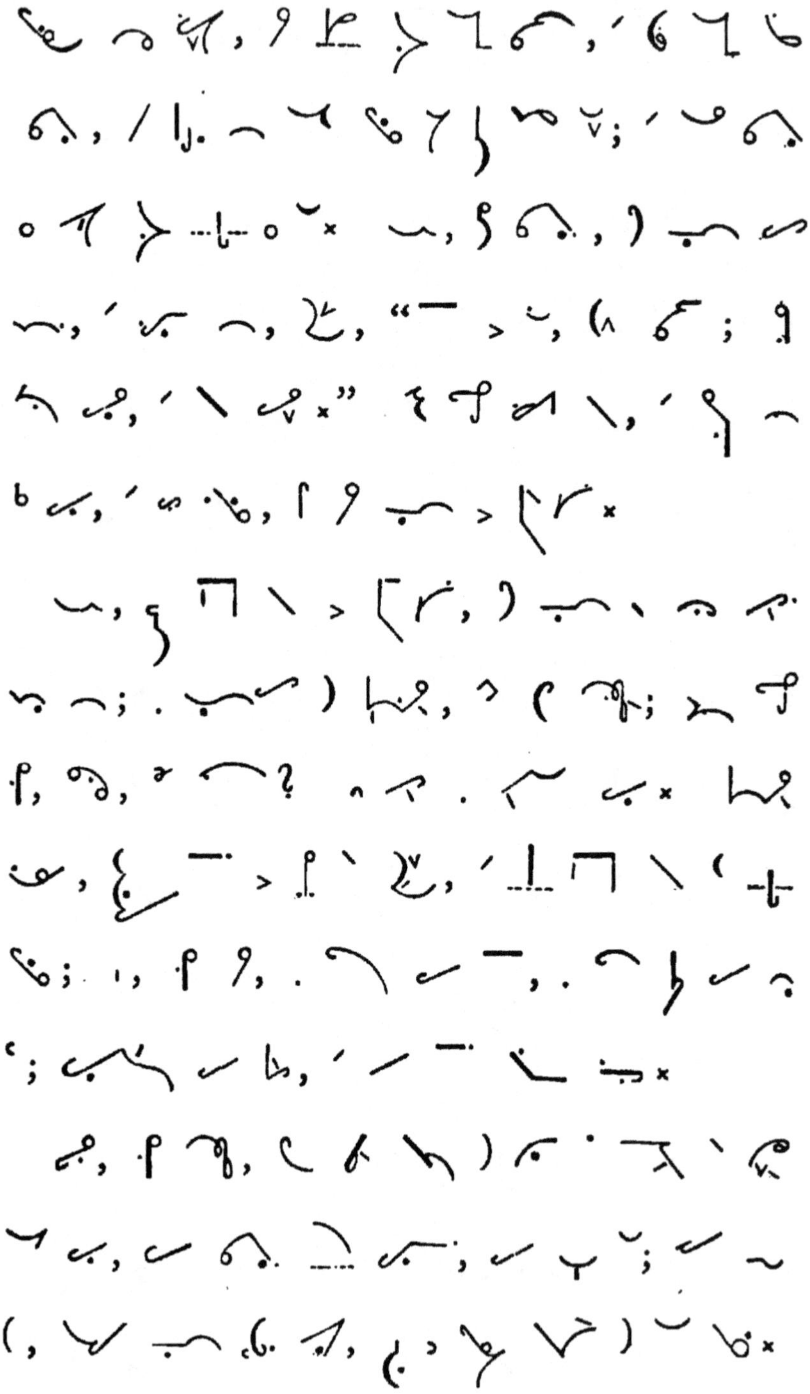

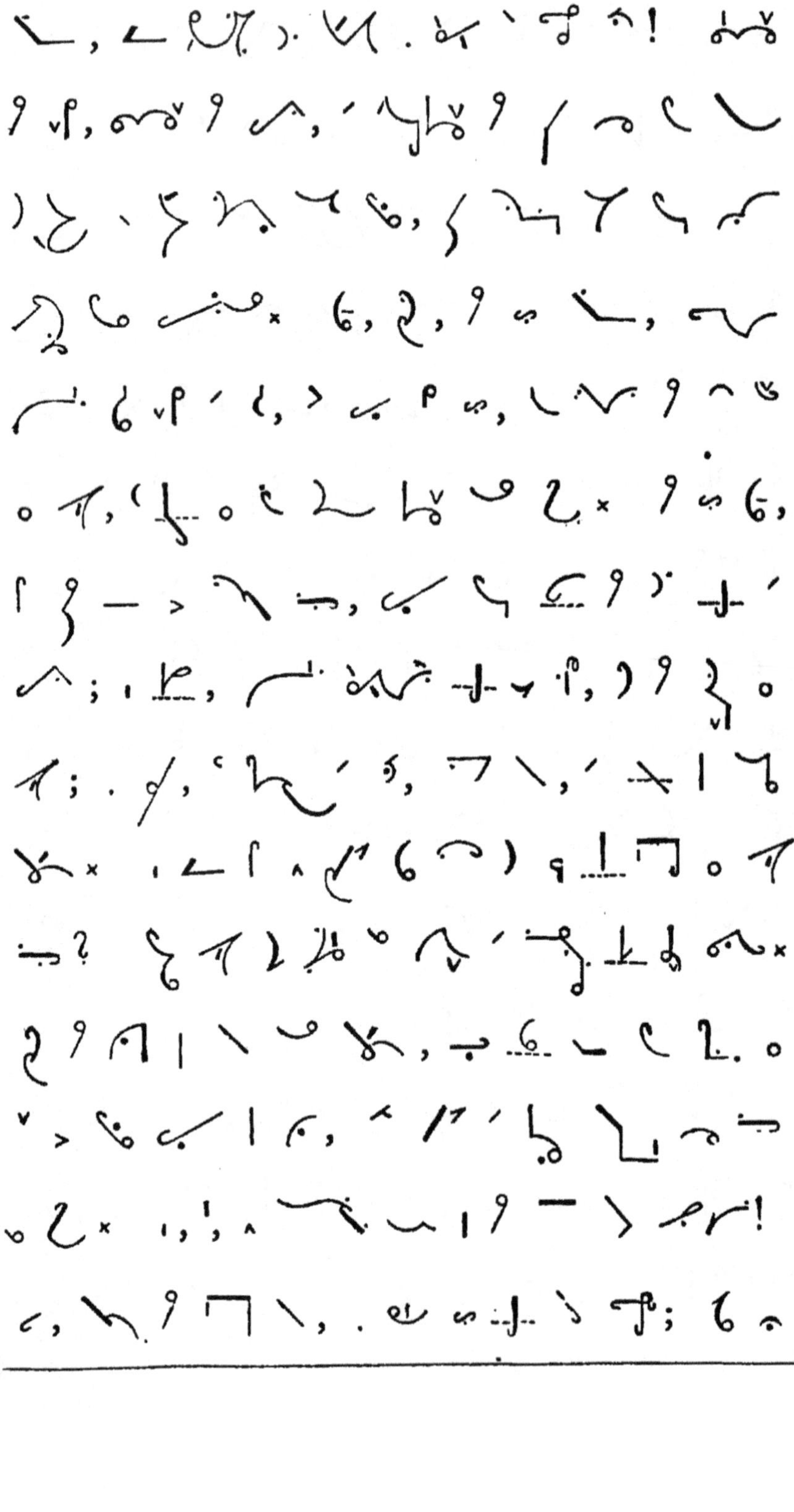

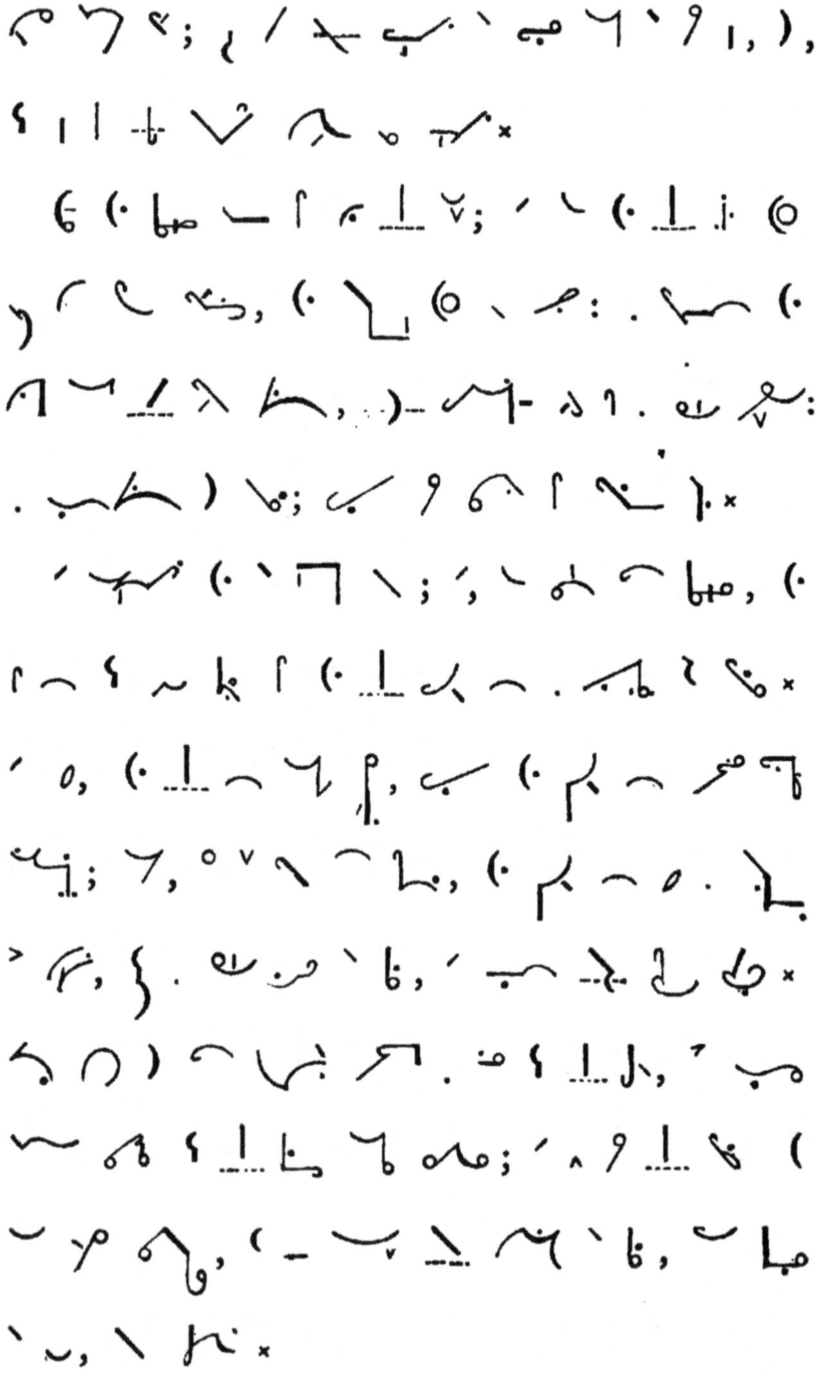

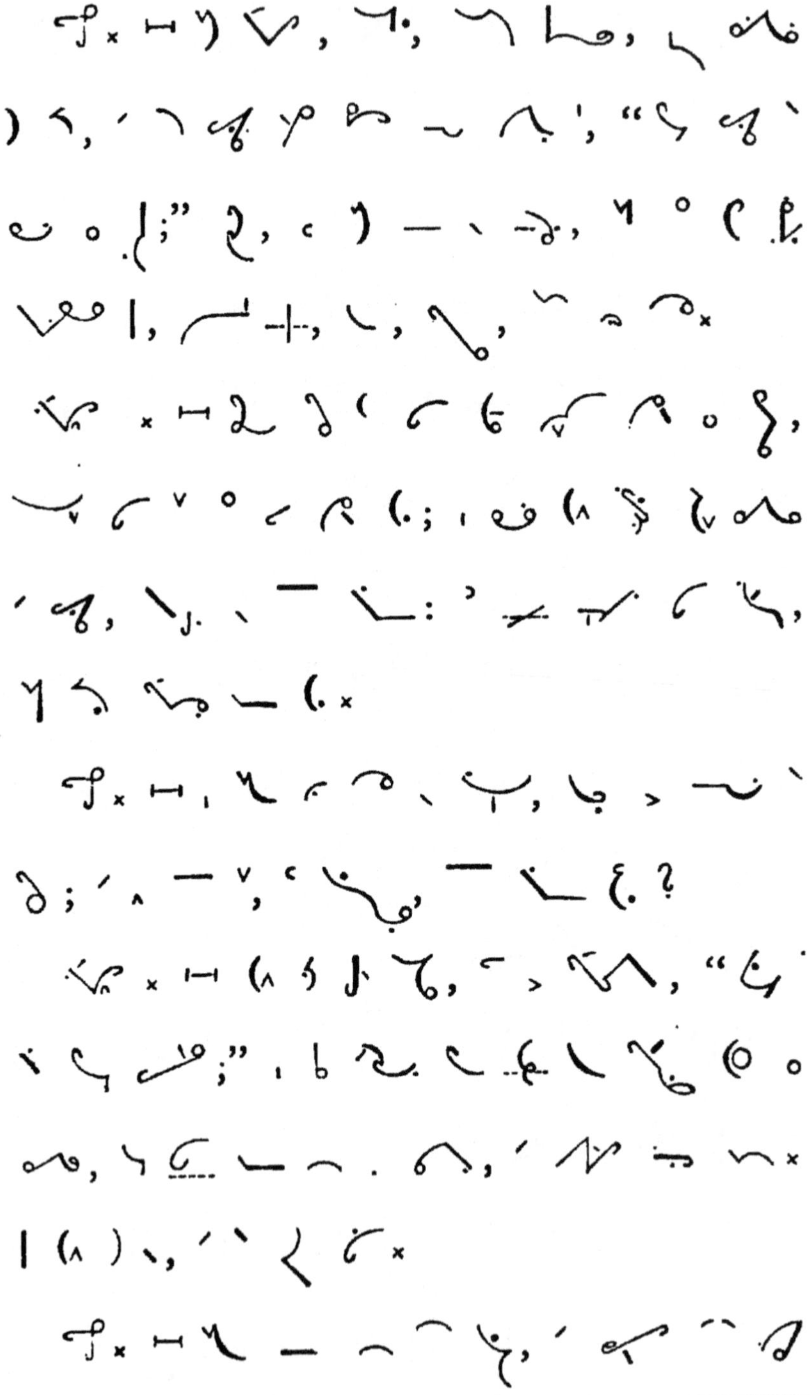

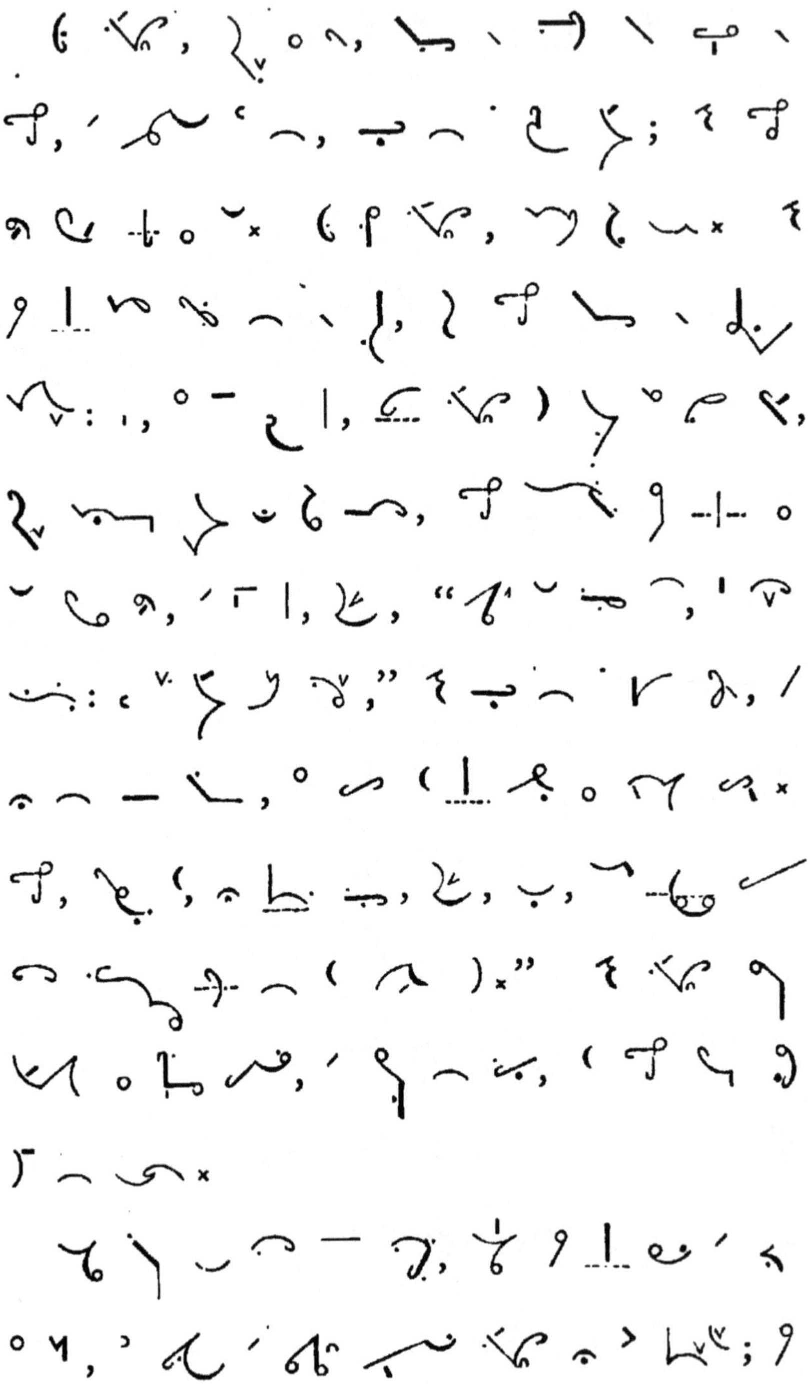

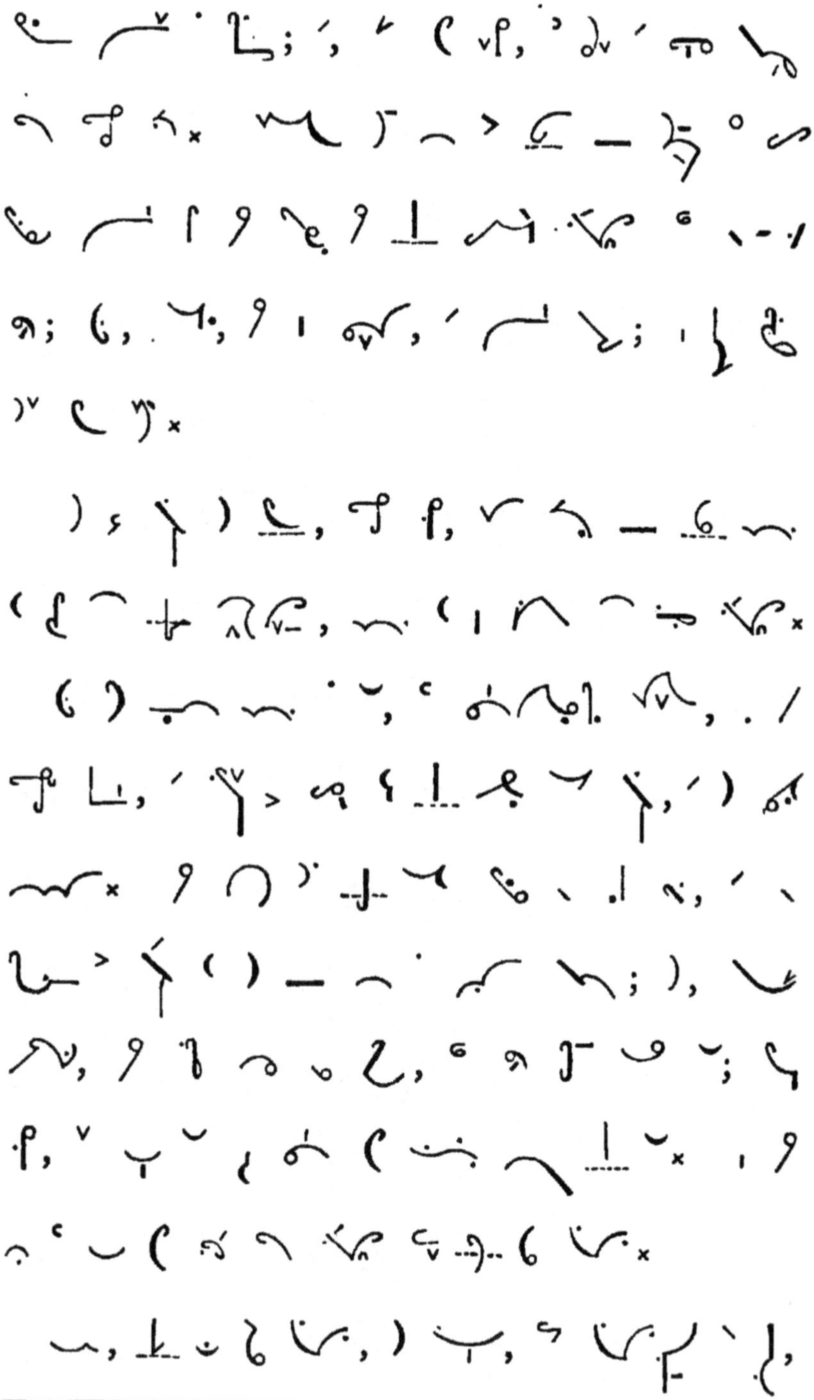

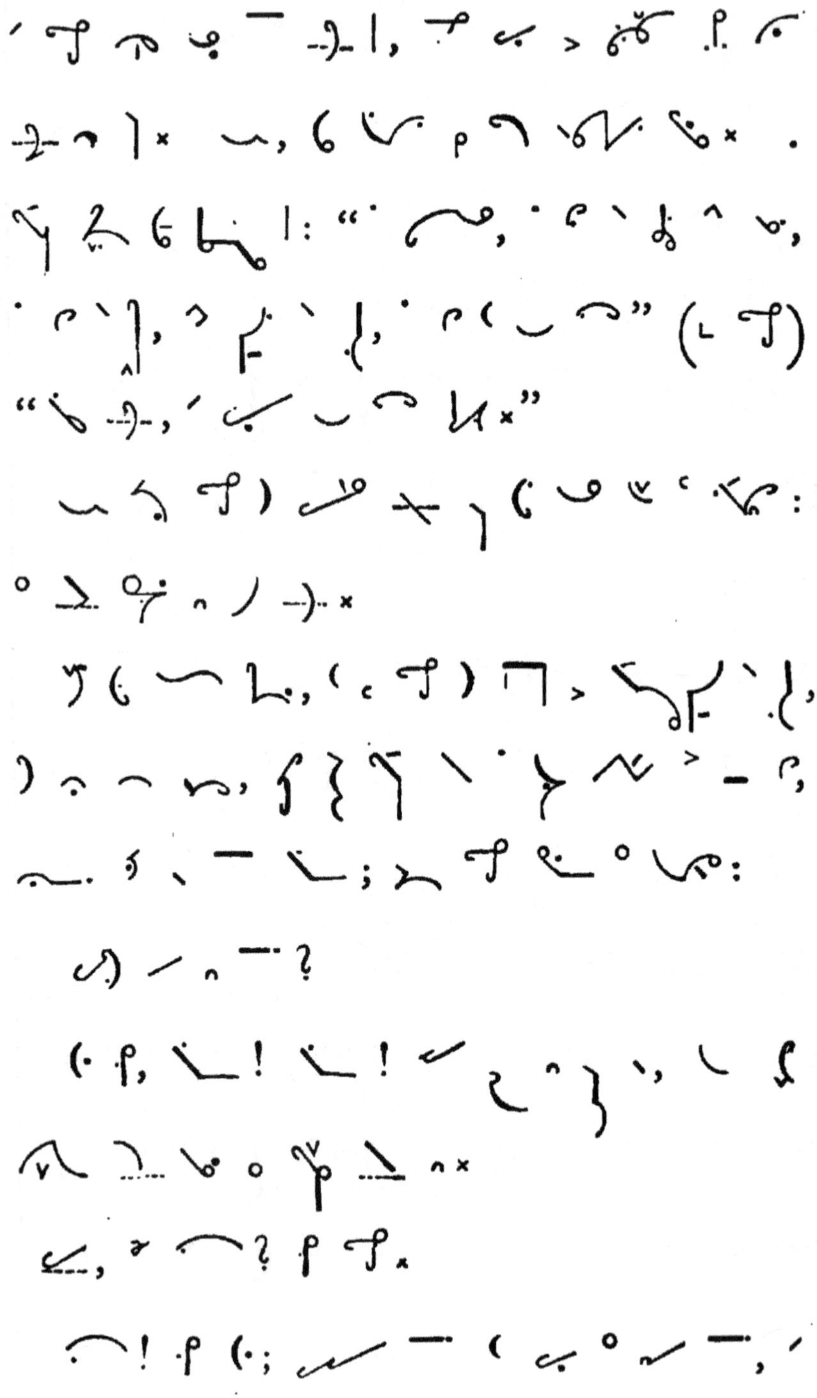

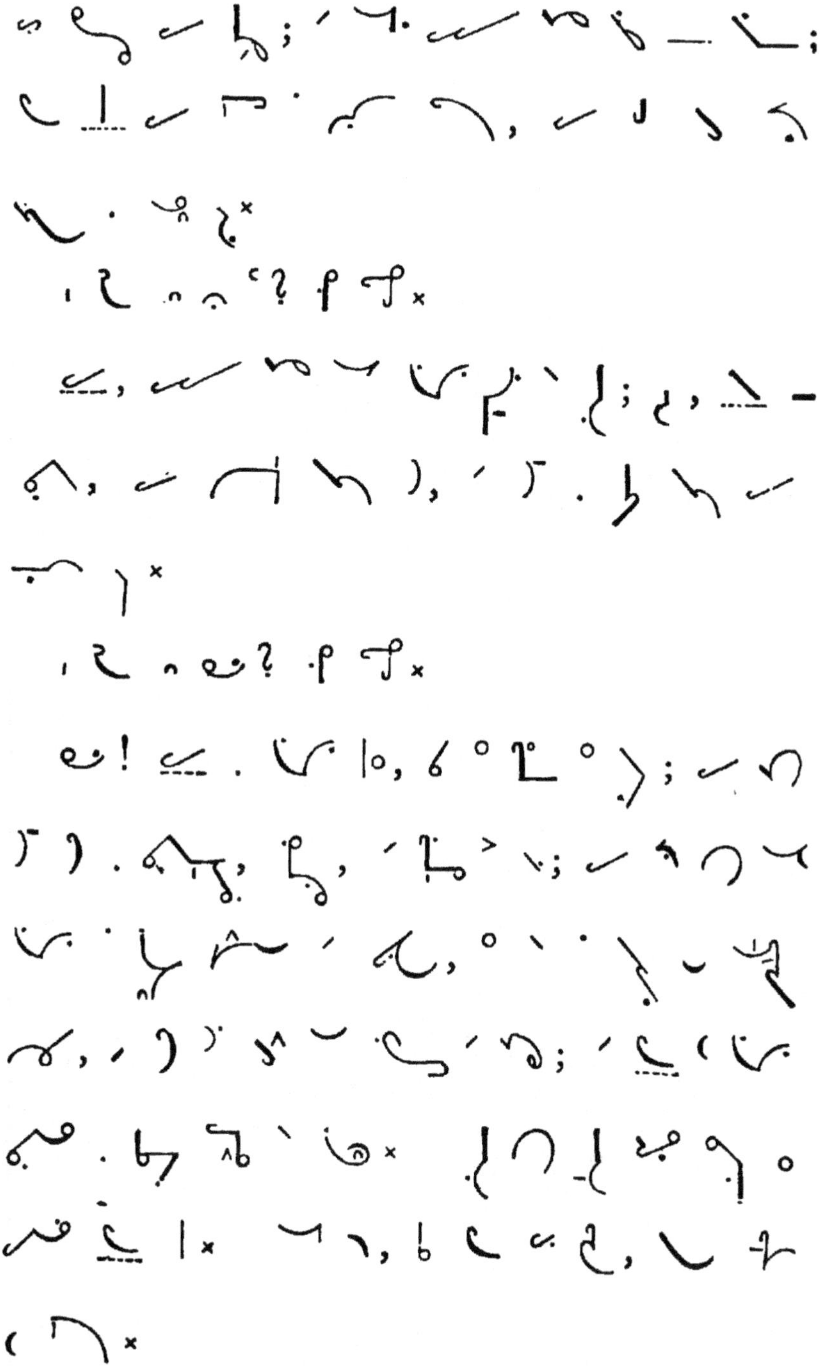

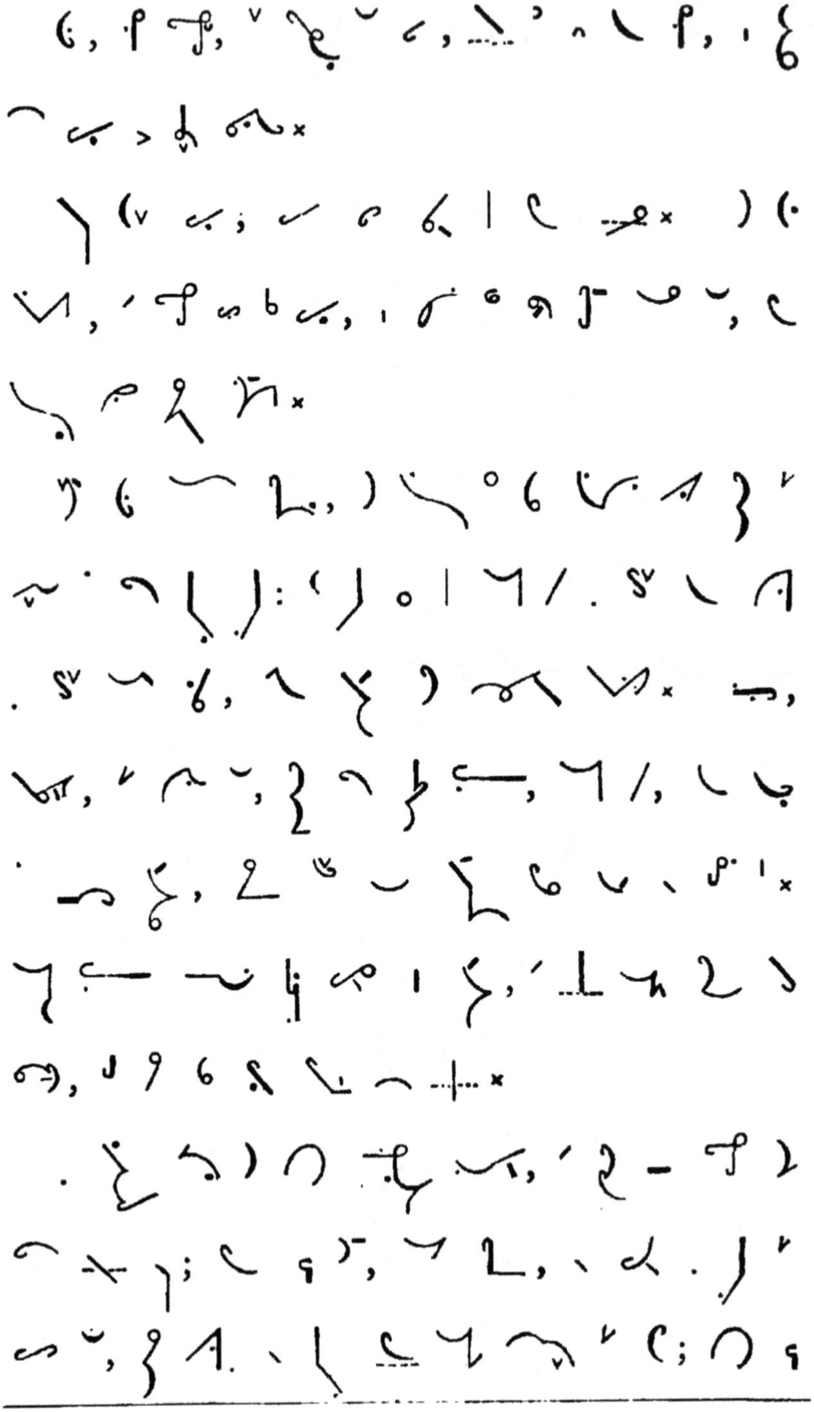

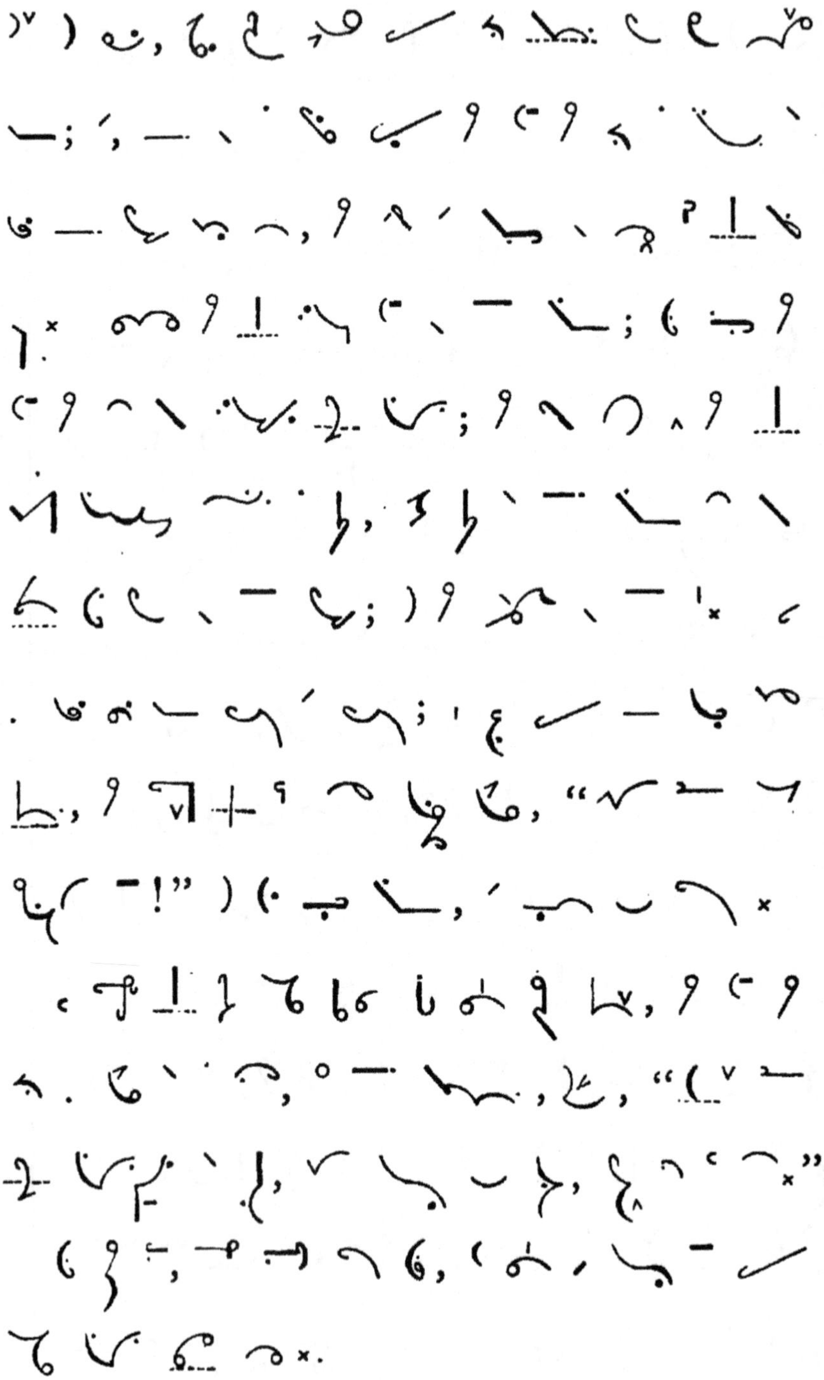

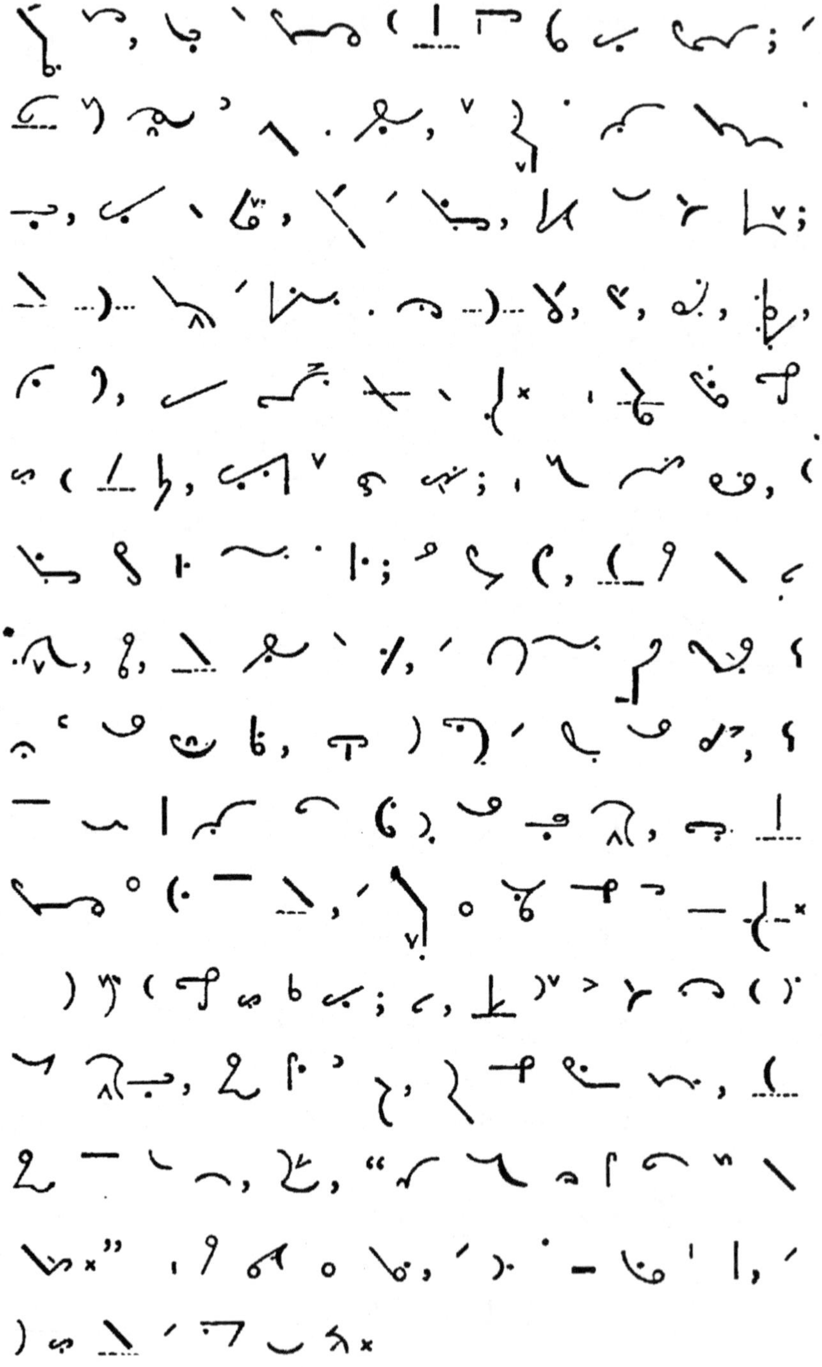

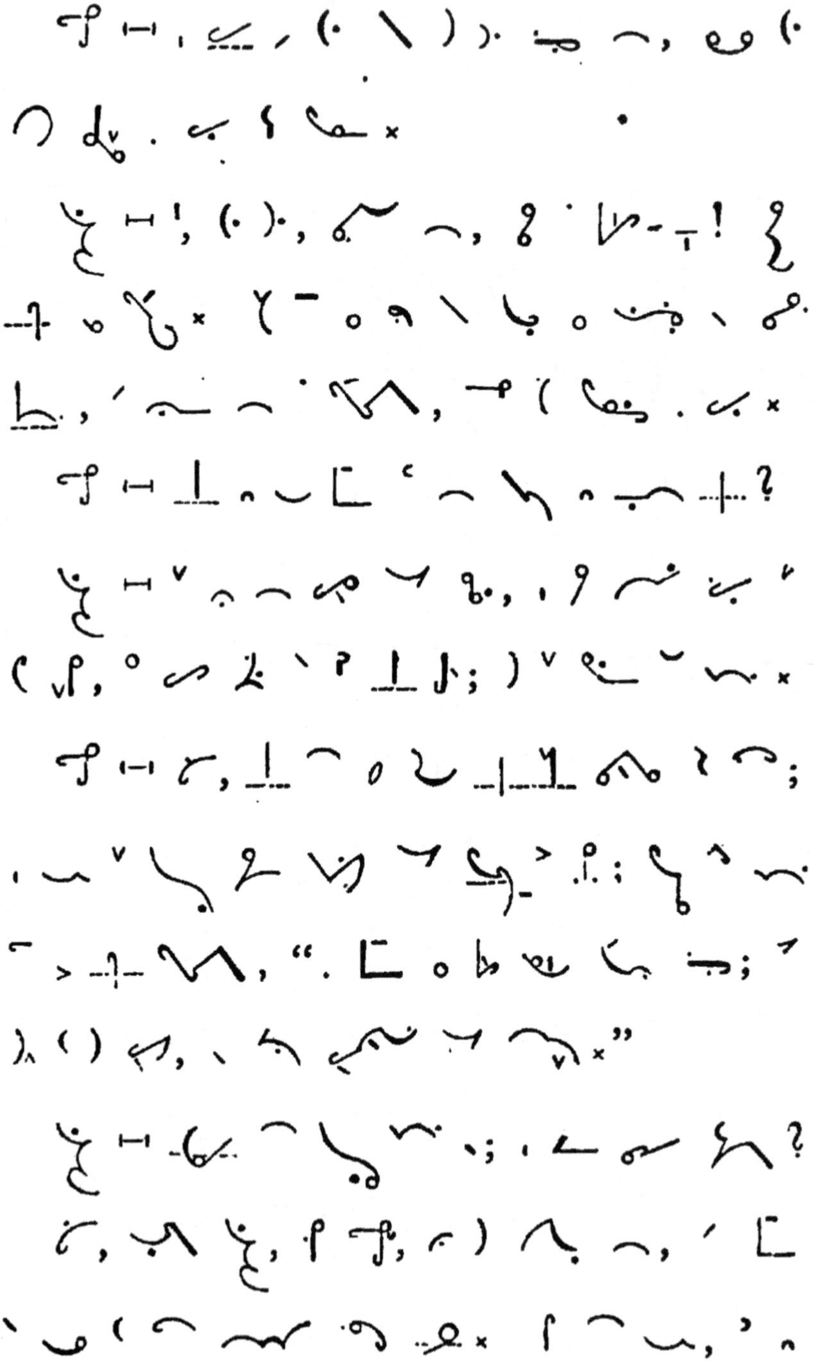

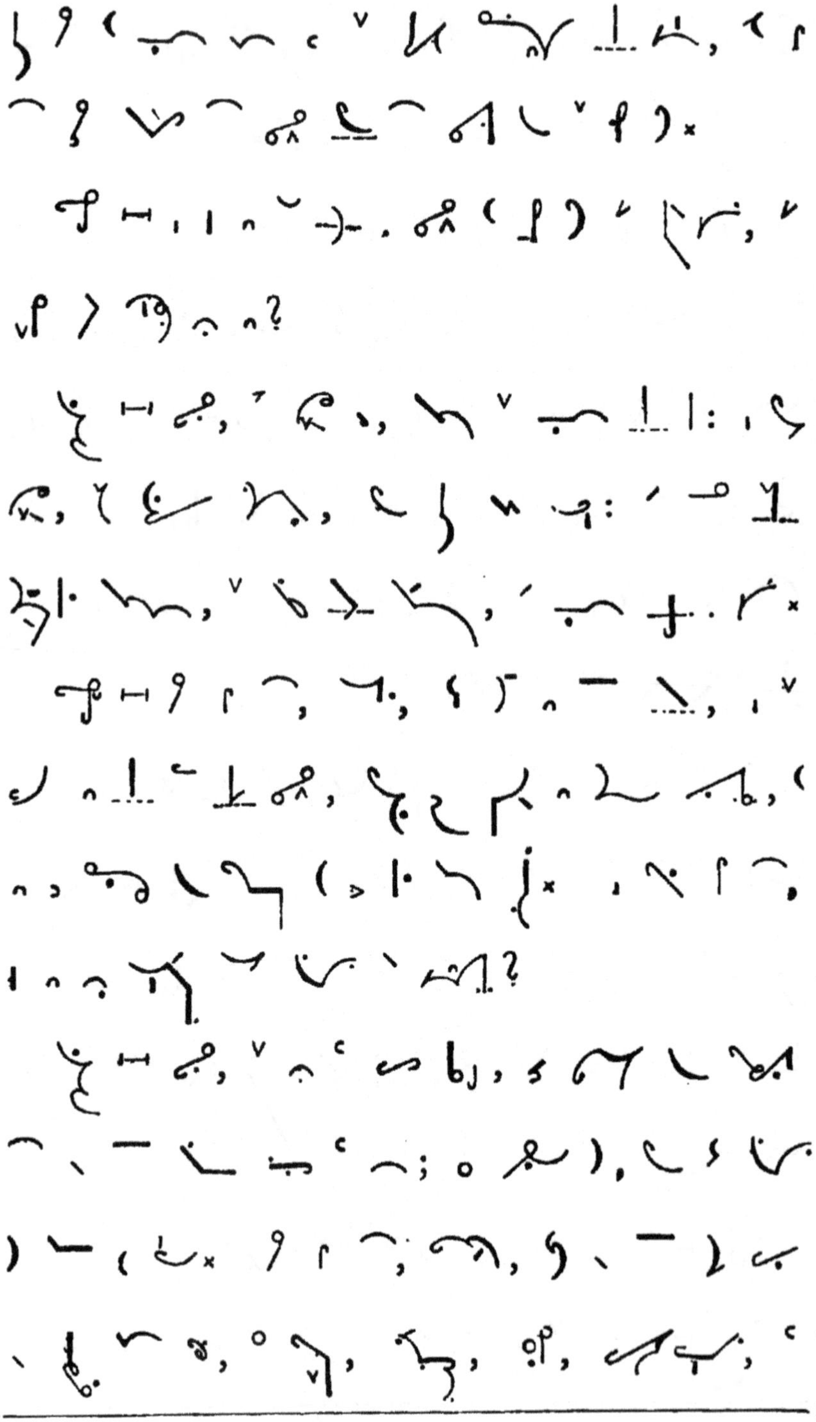

(Shorthand text — not transcribable as Latin characters.)

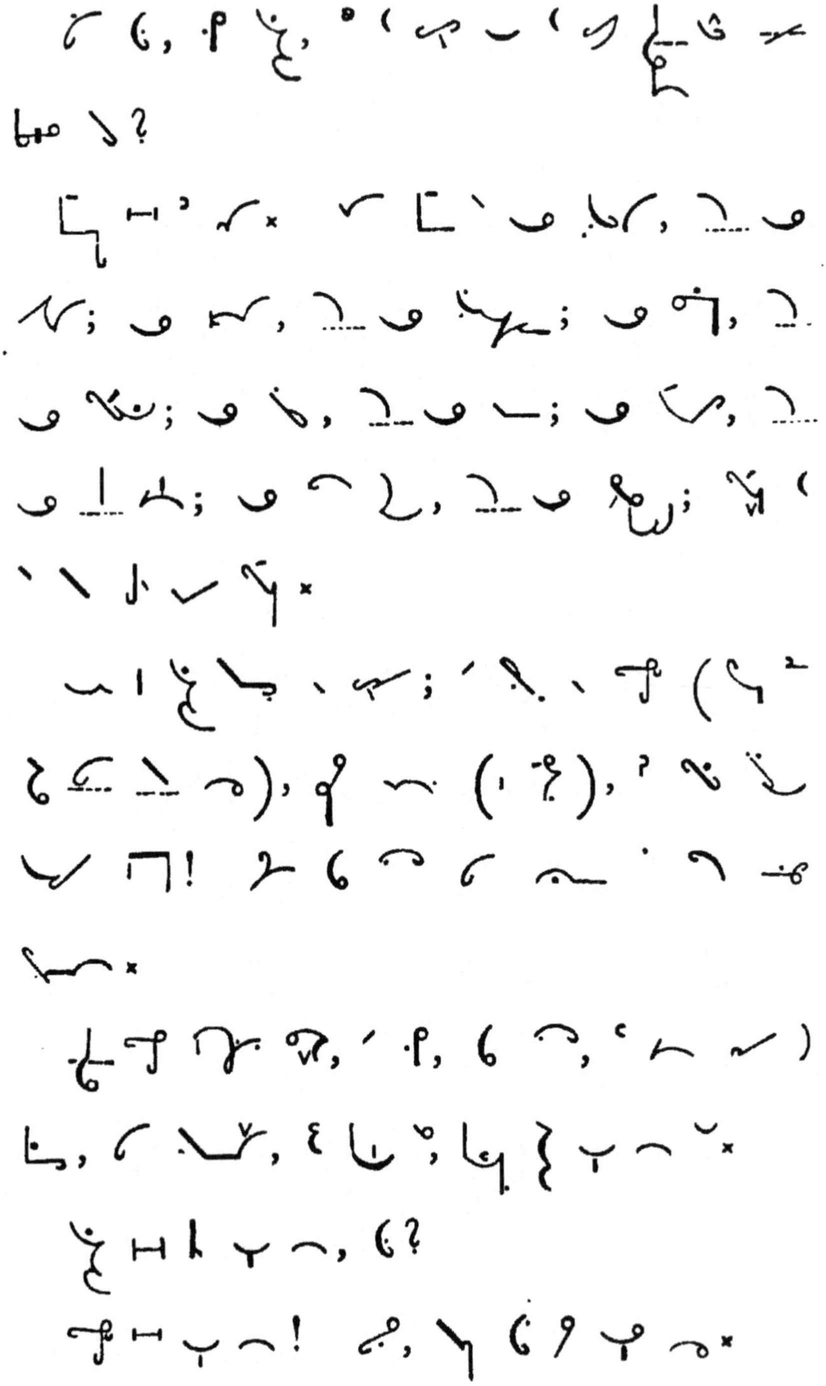

[Shorthand text - not transcribable]

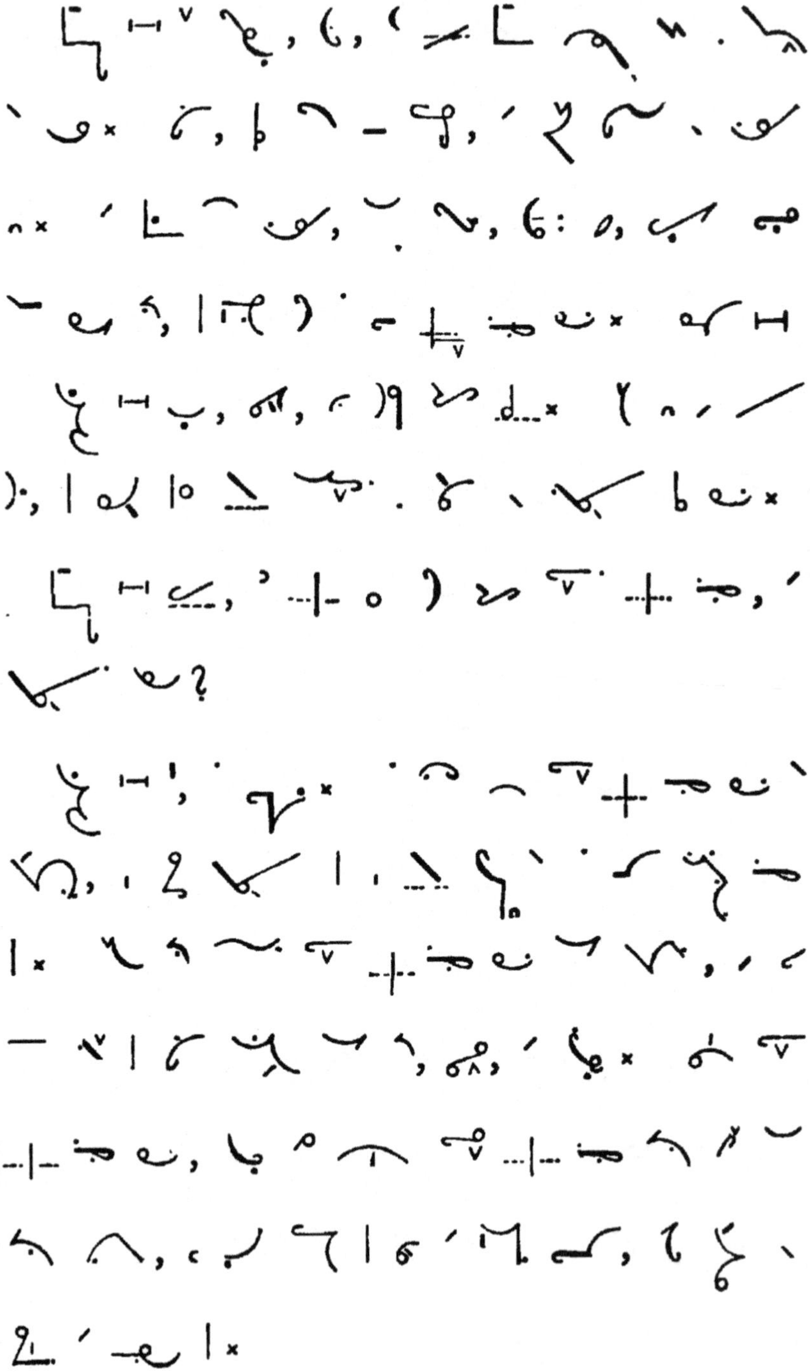

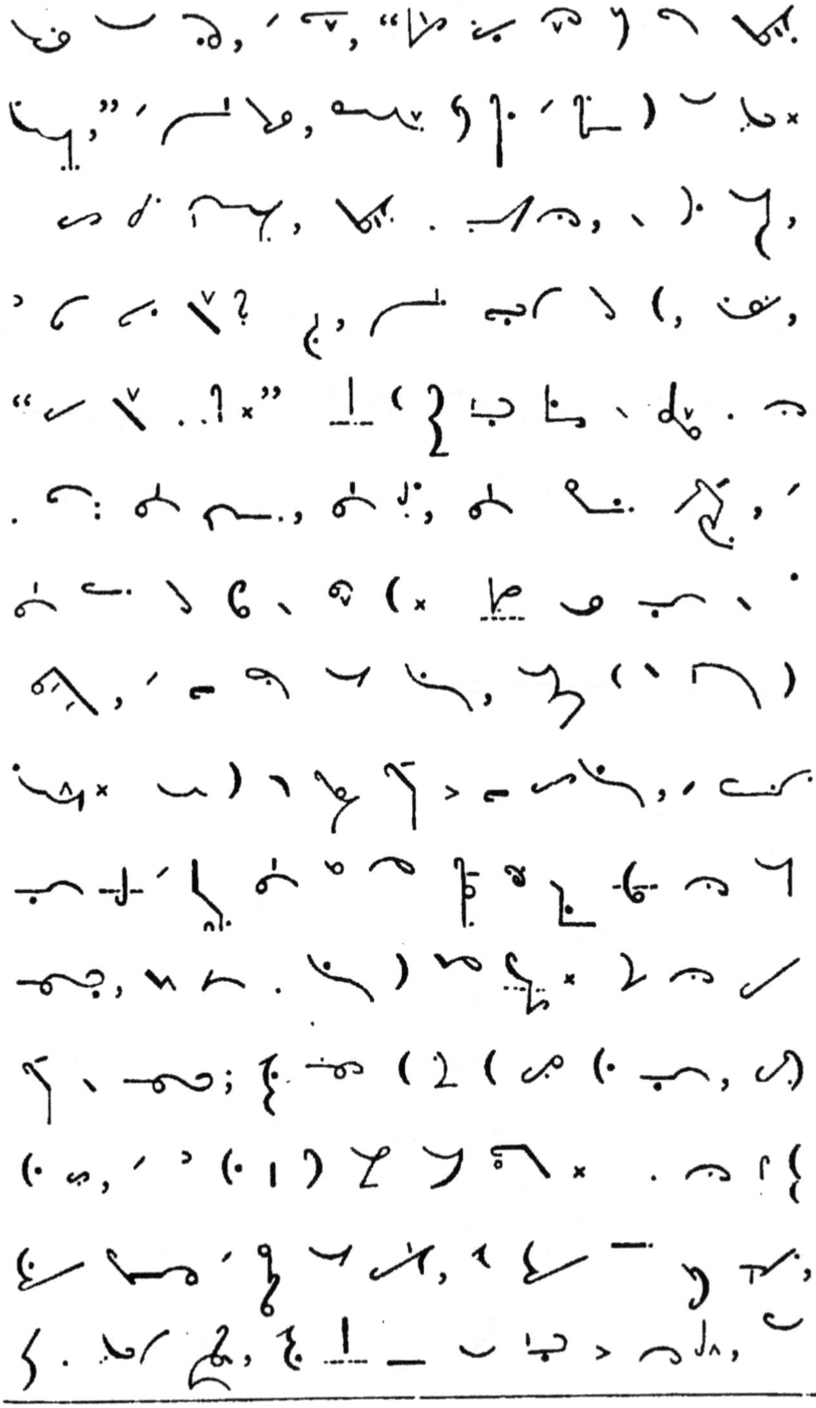

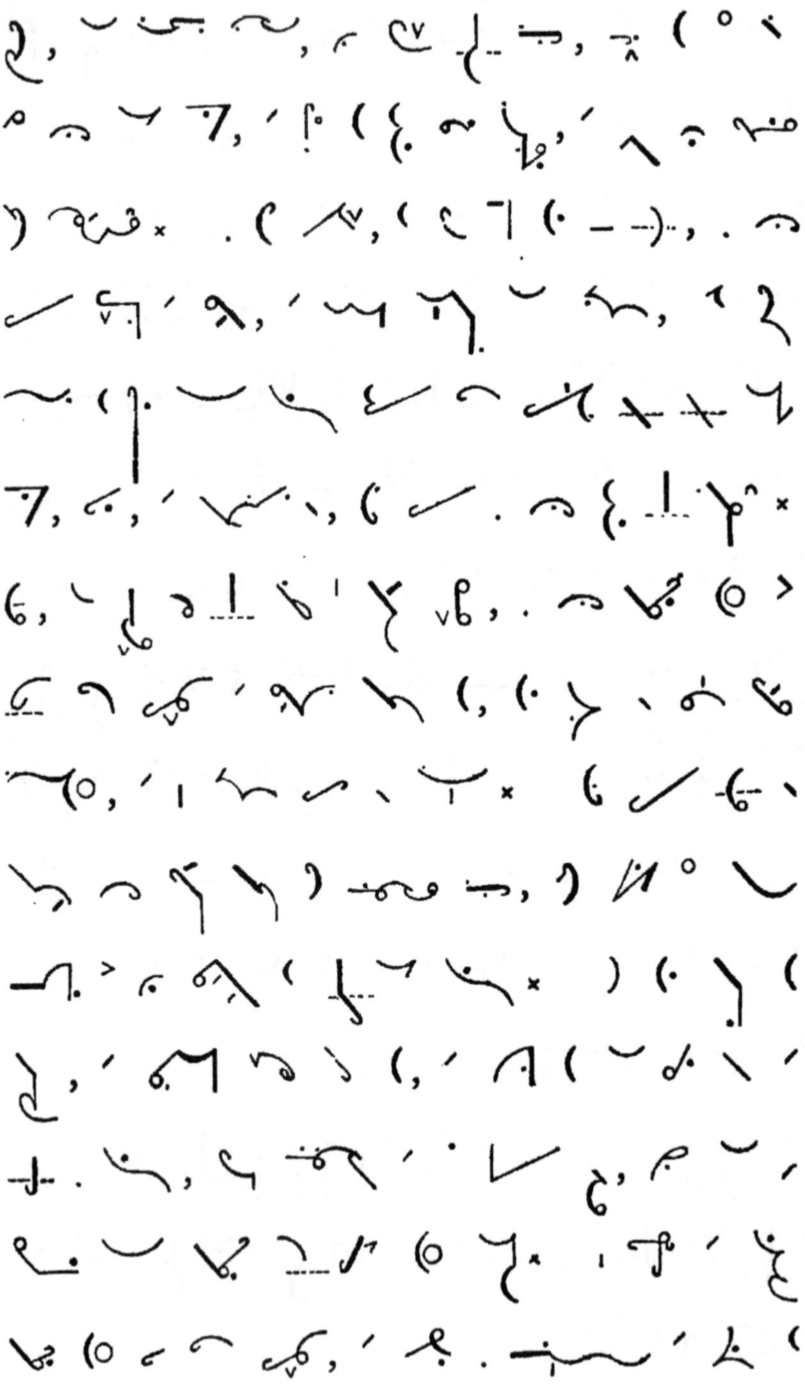

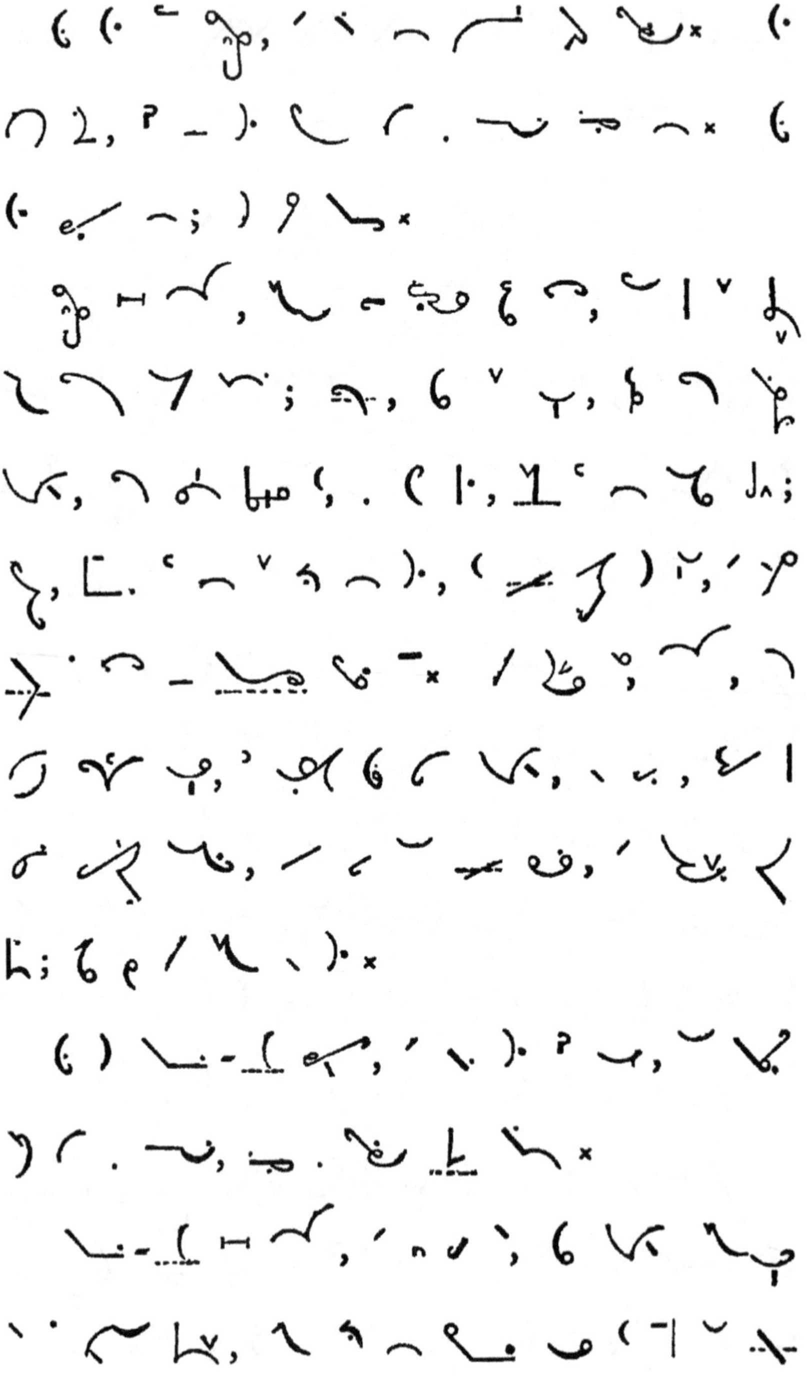

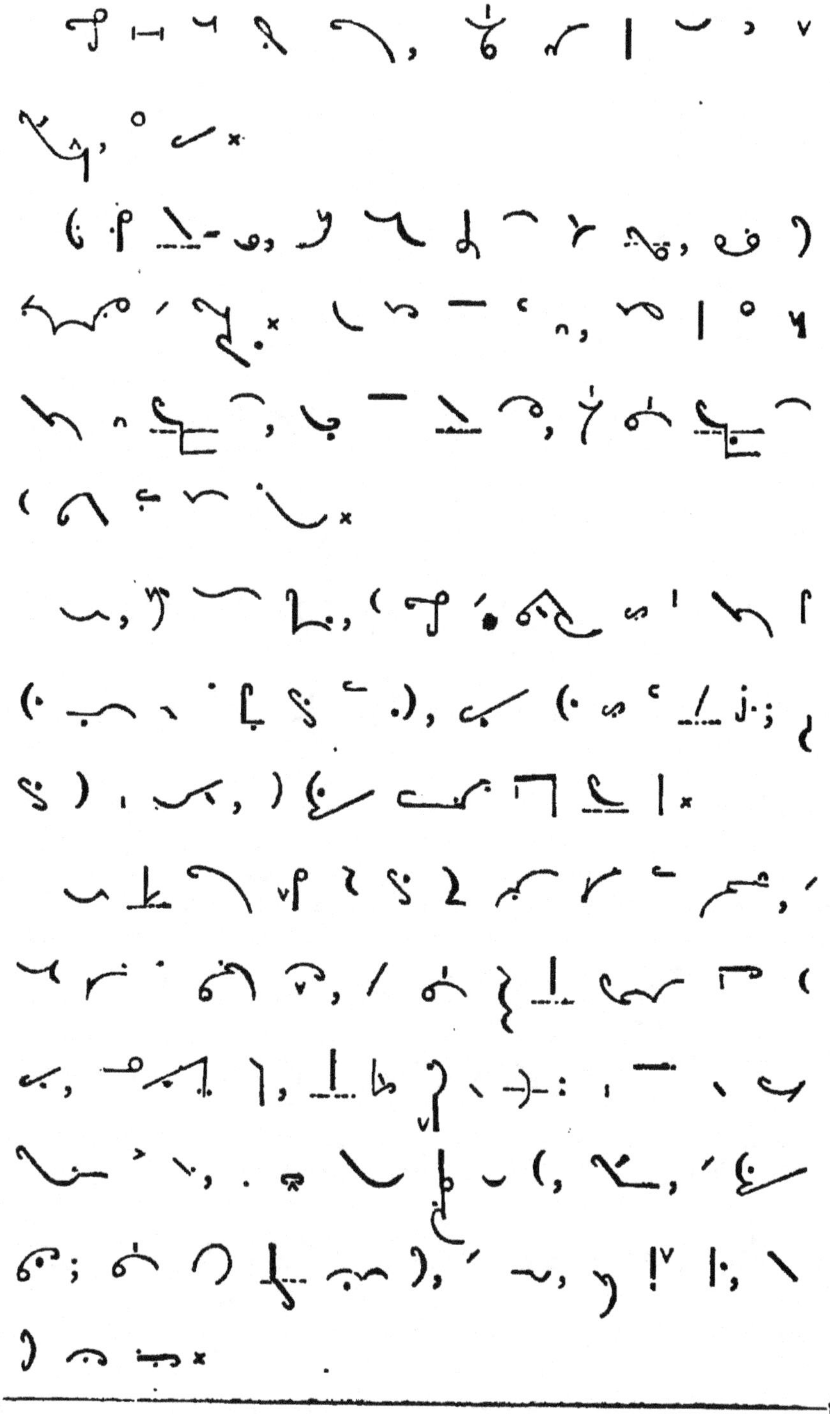

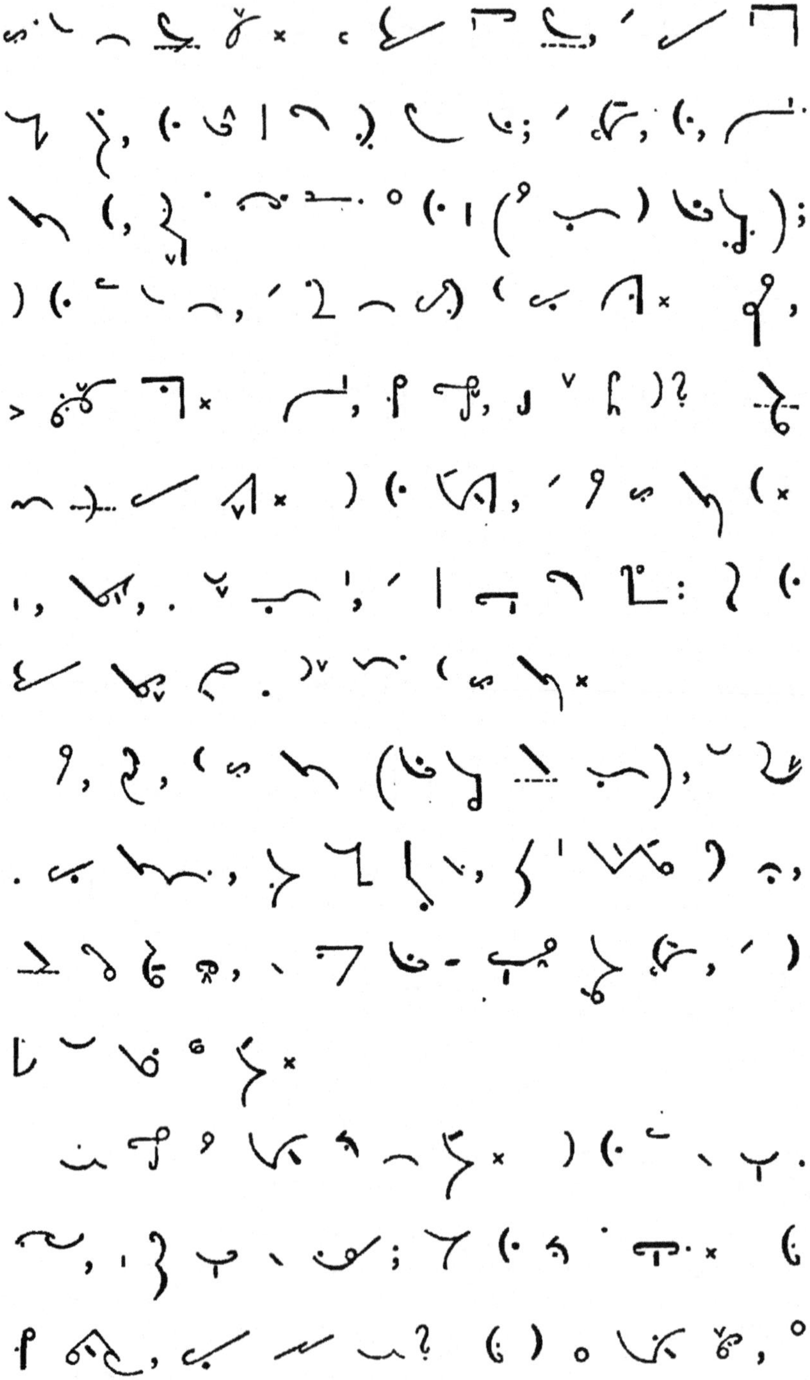

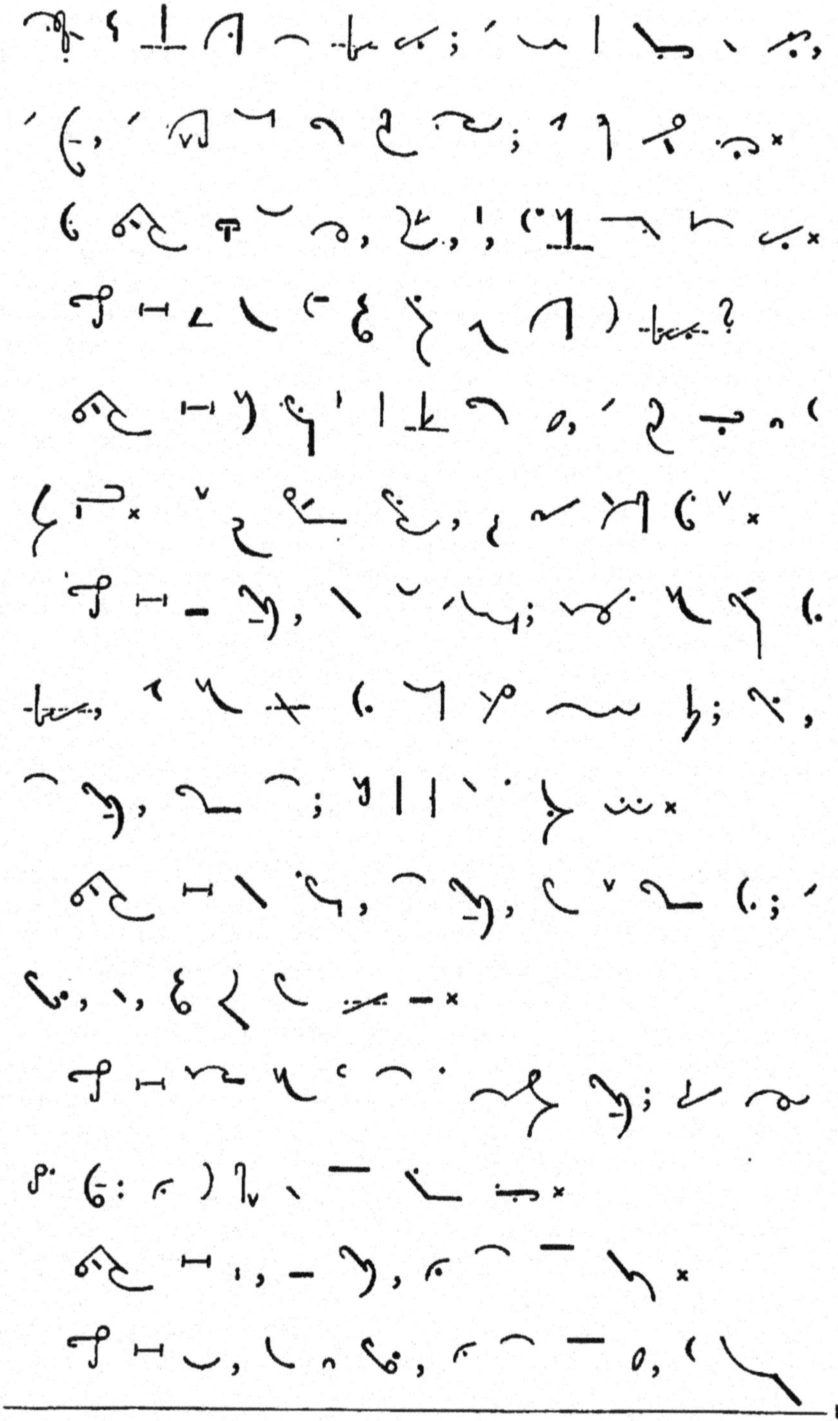

[shorthand text]

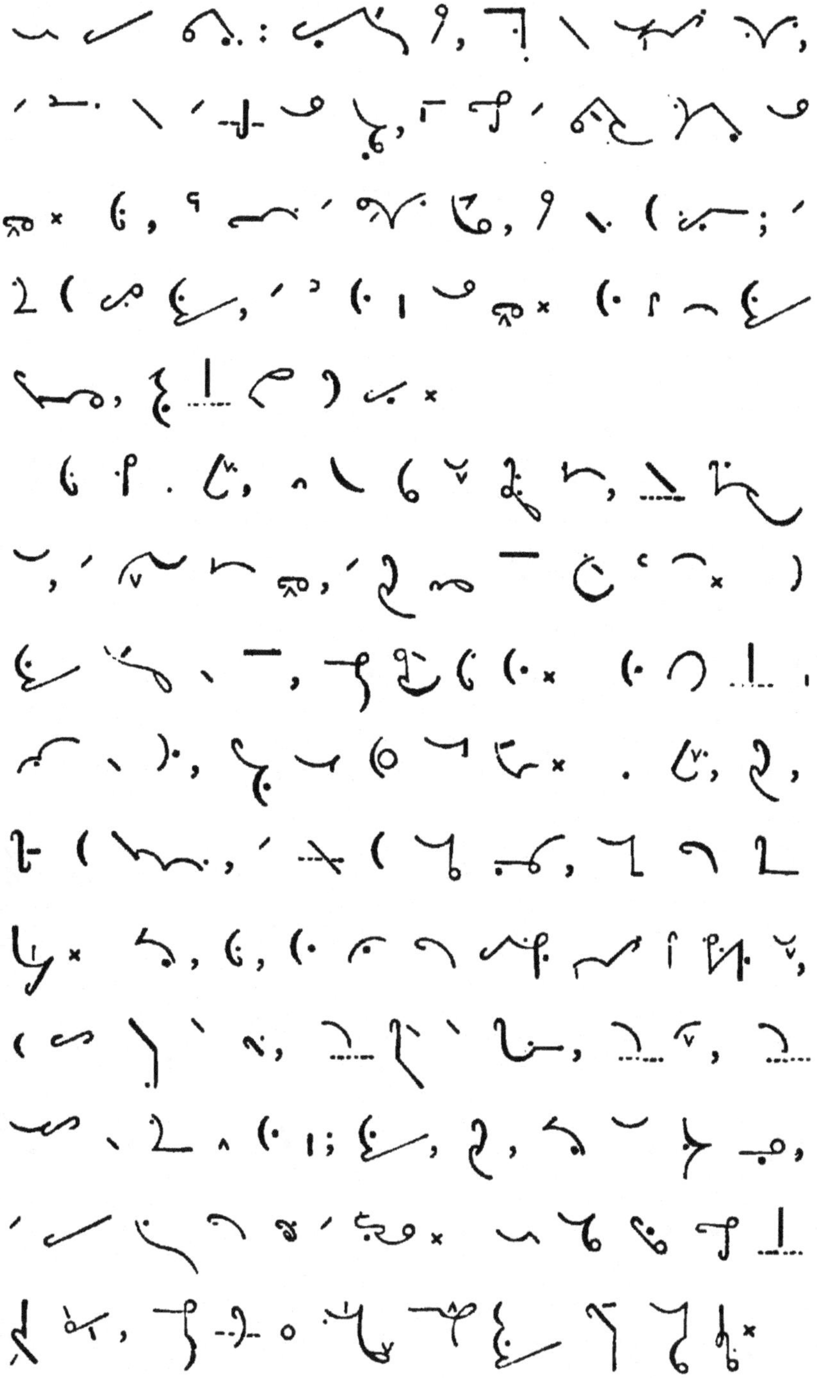

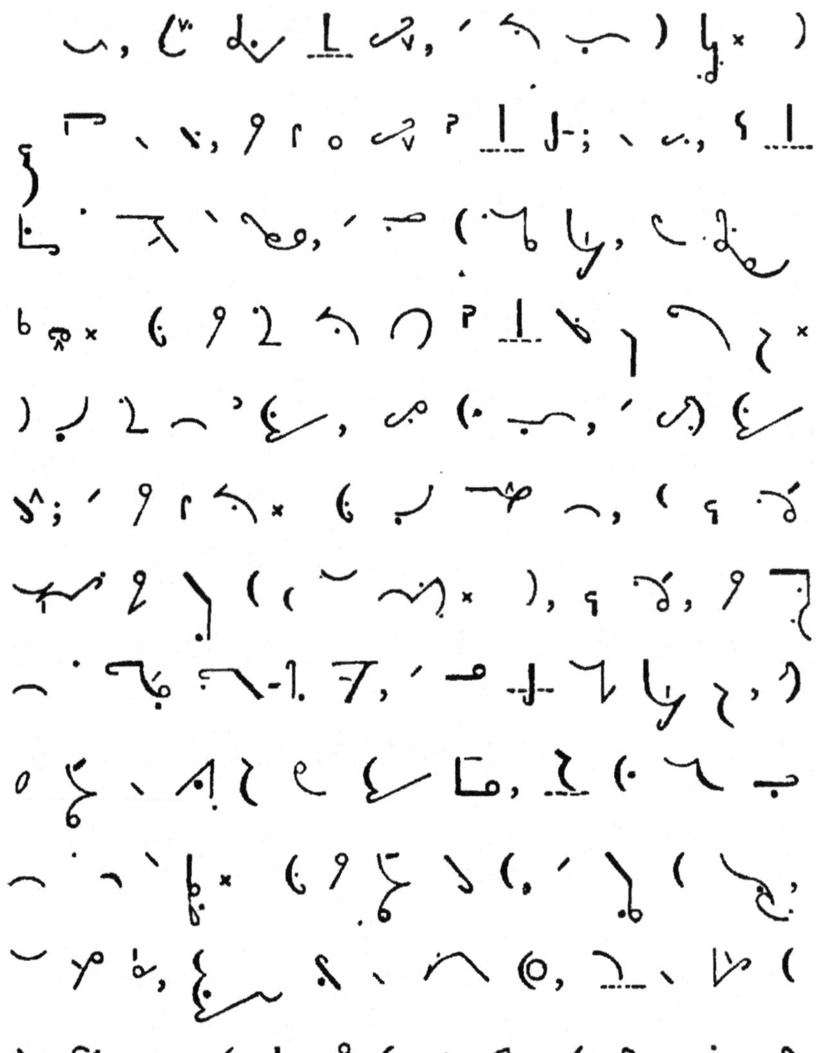

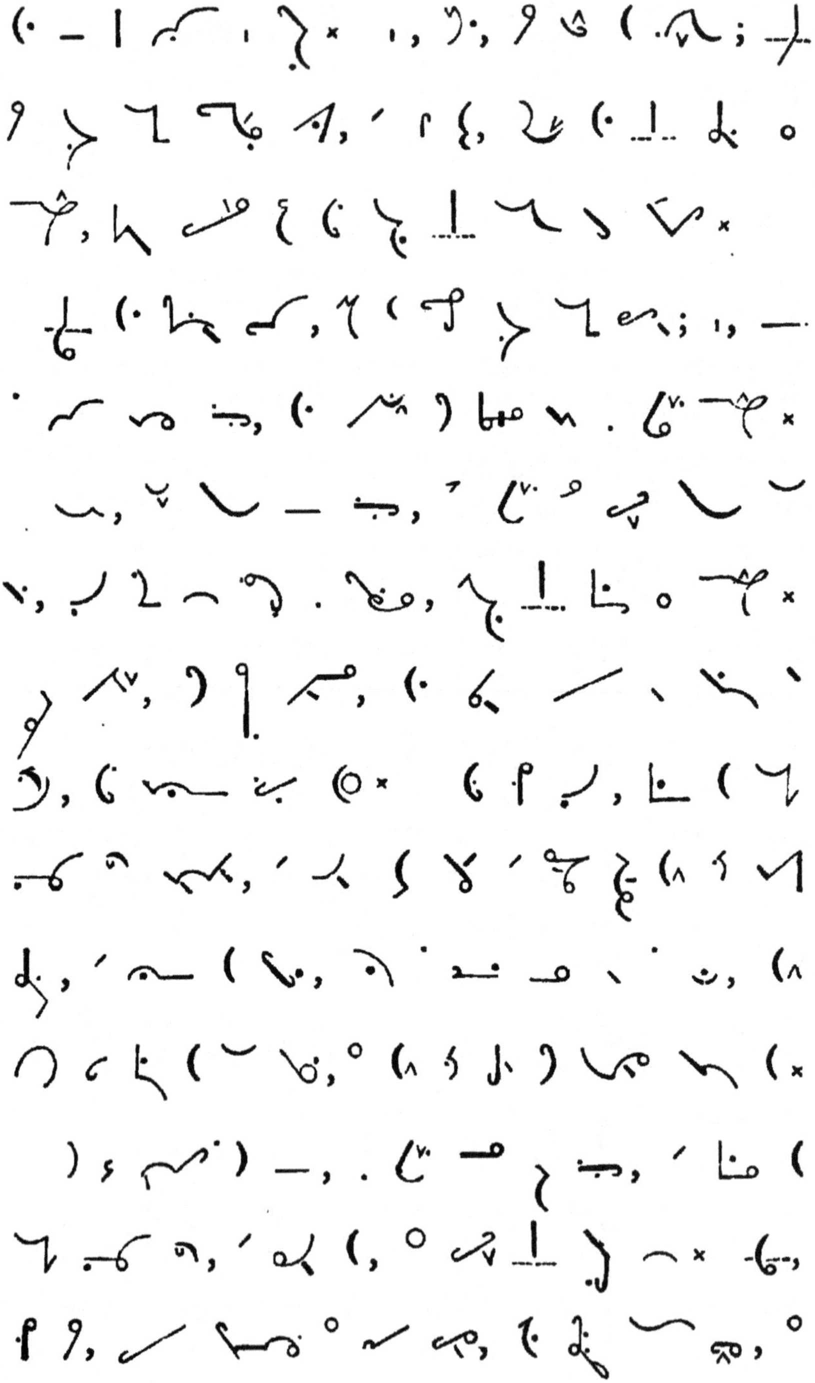

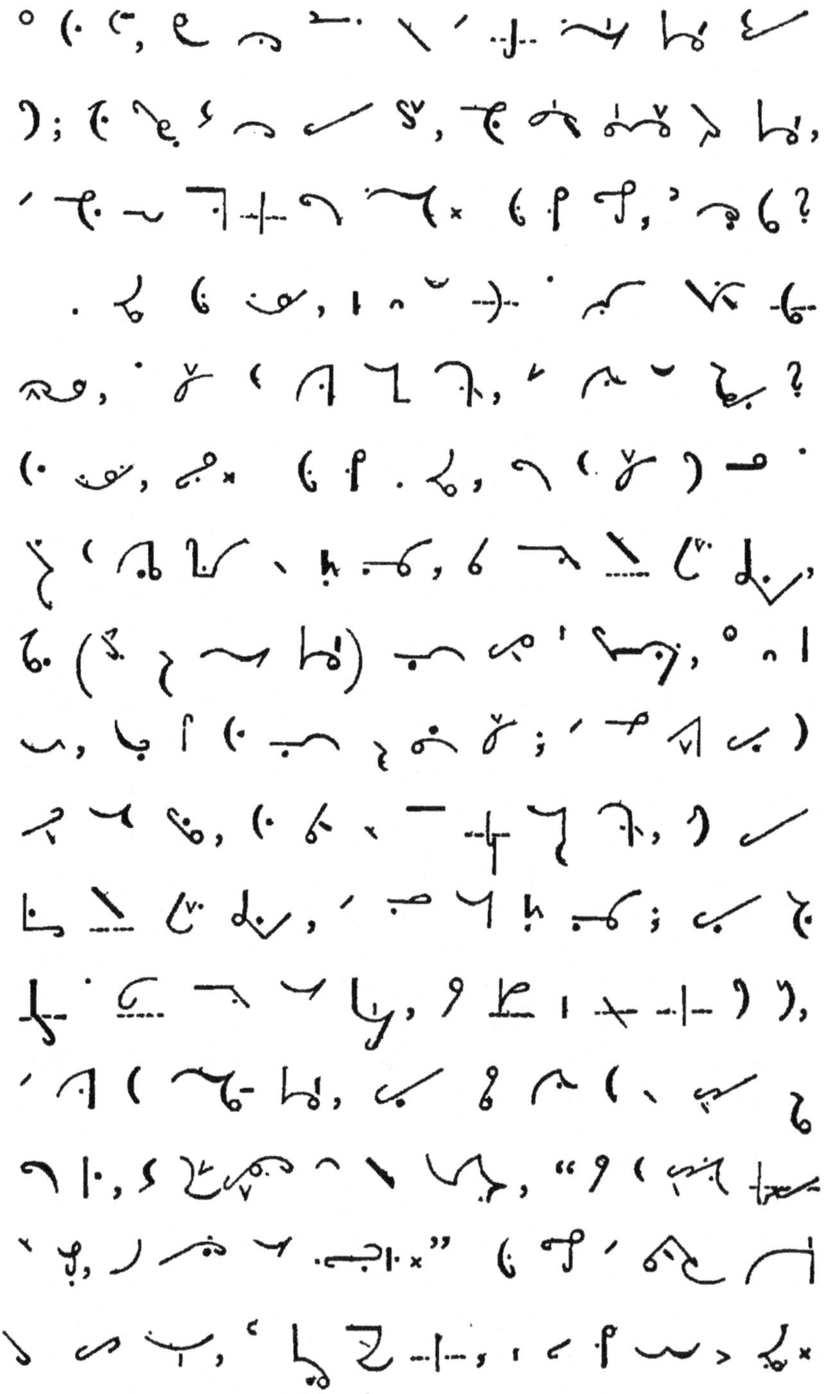

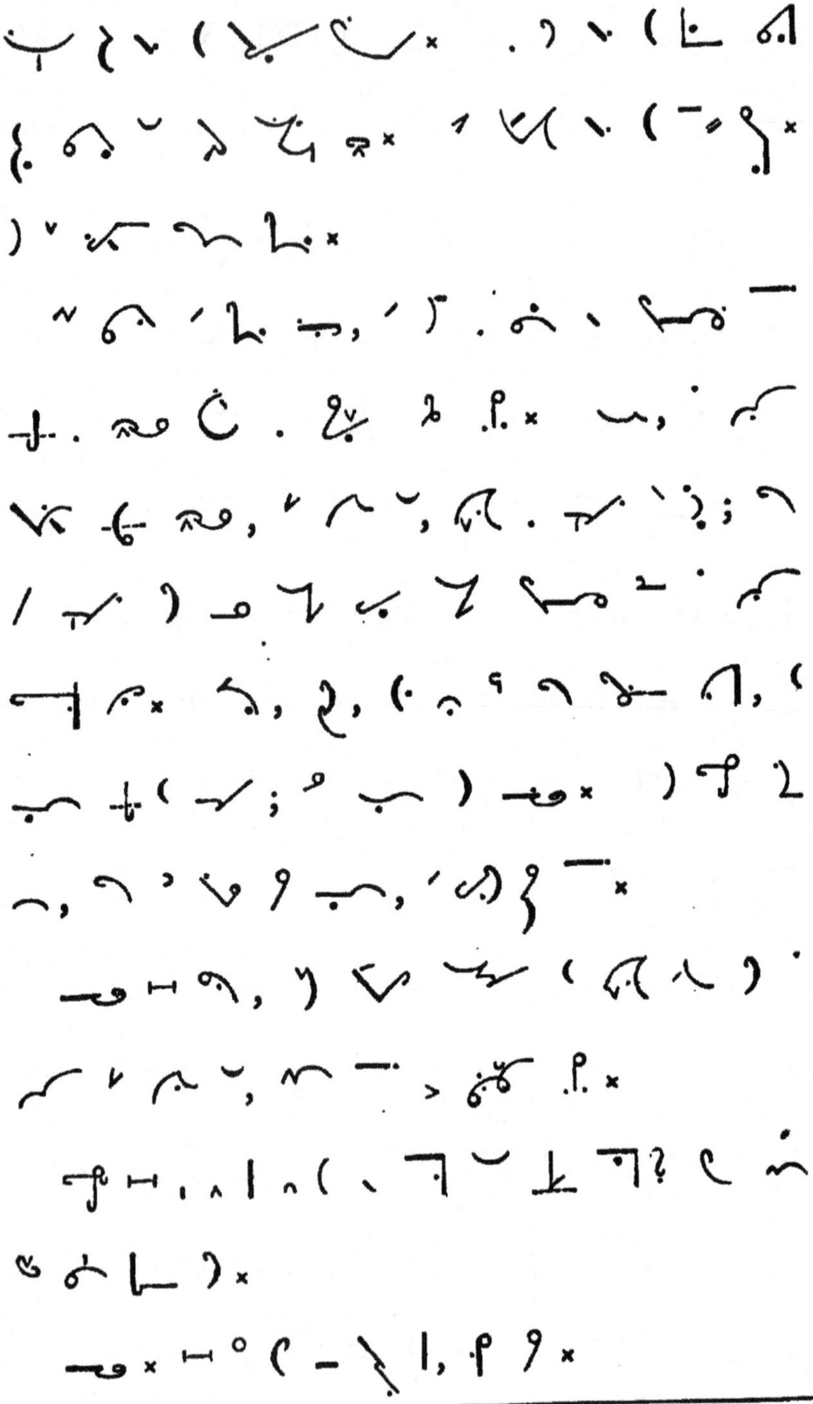

[Page of shorthand symbols - not transcribable as text]

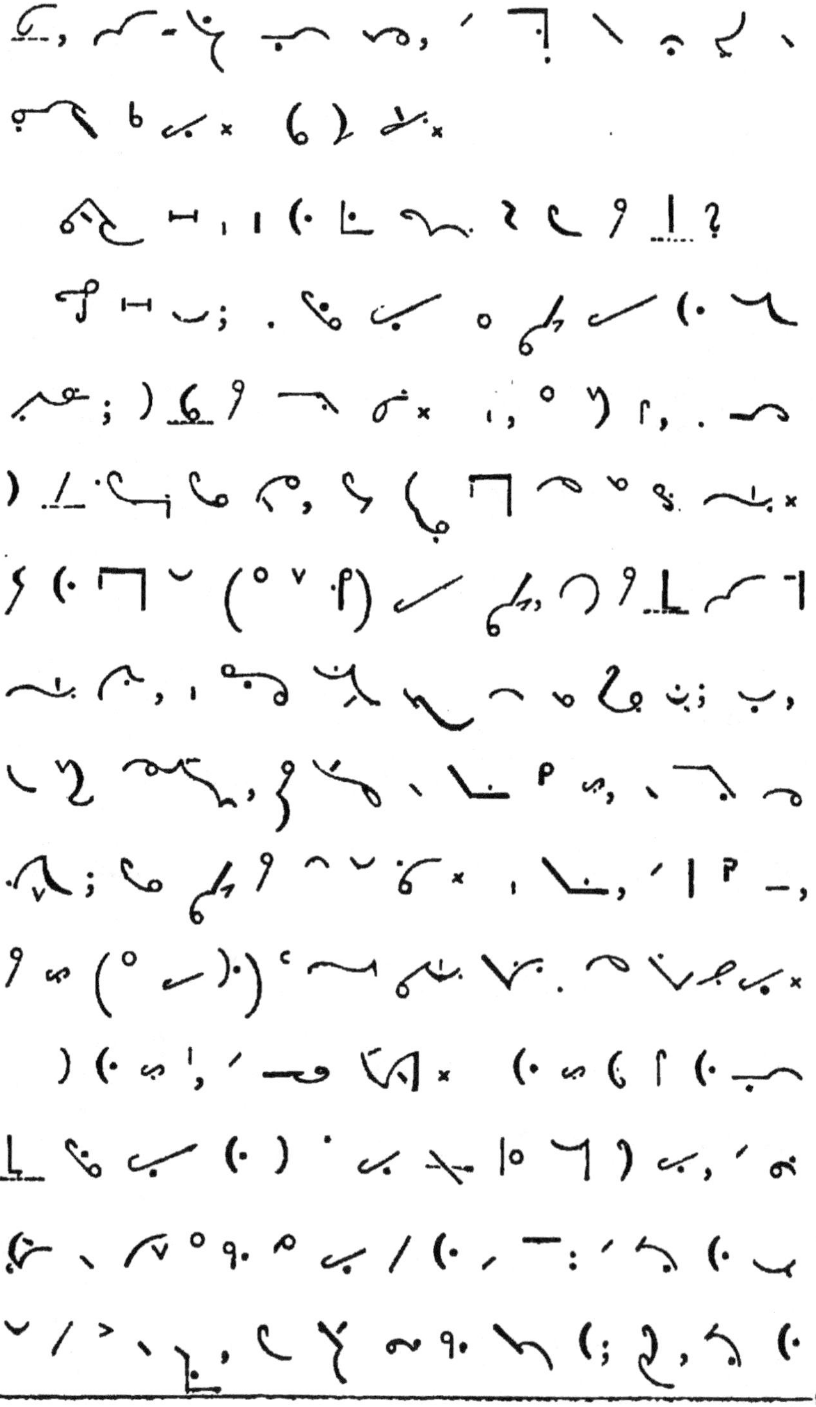

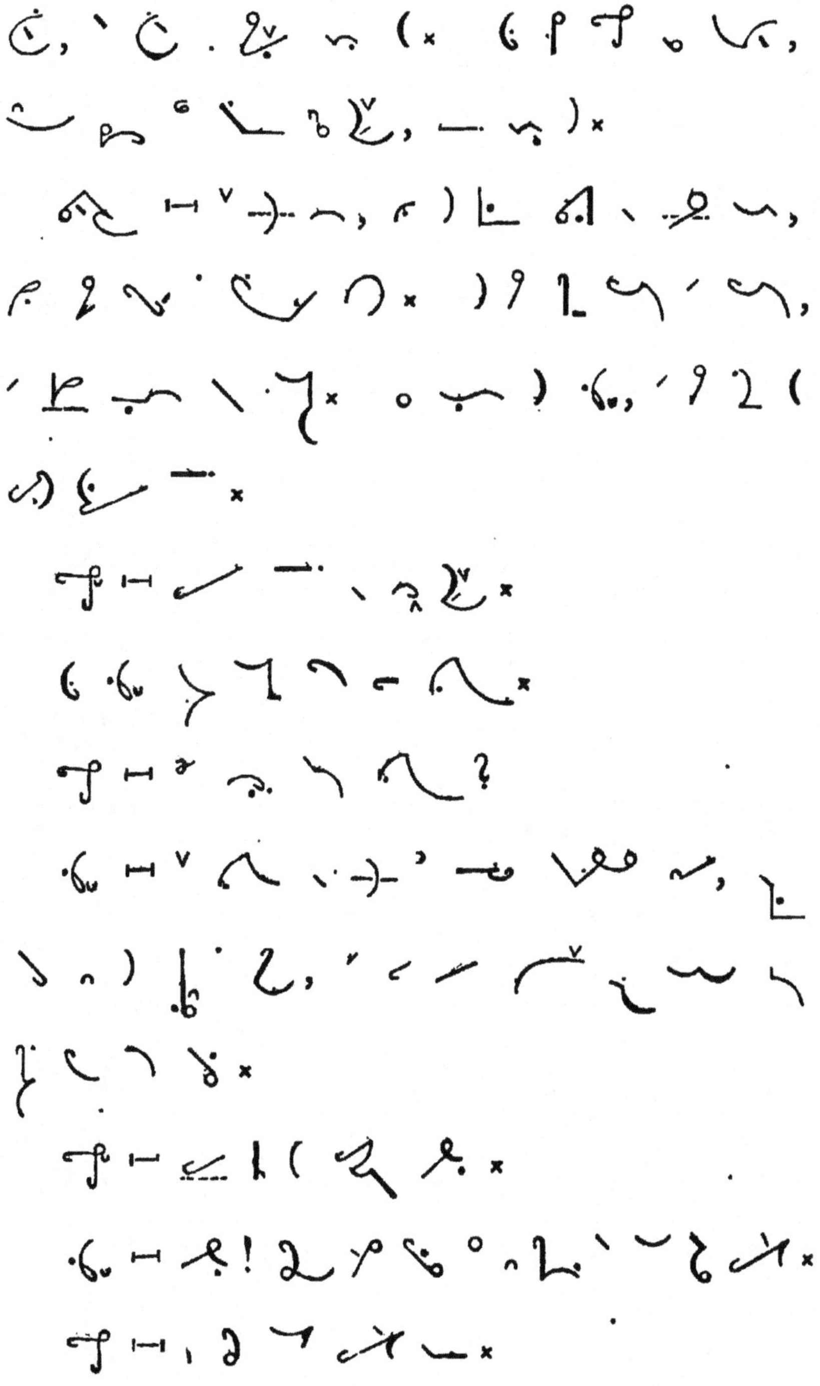

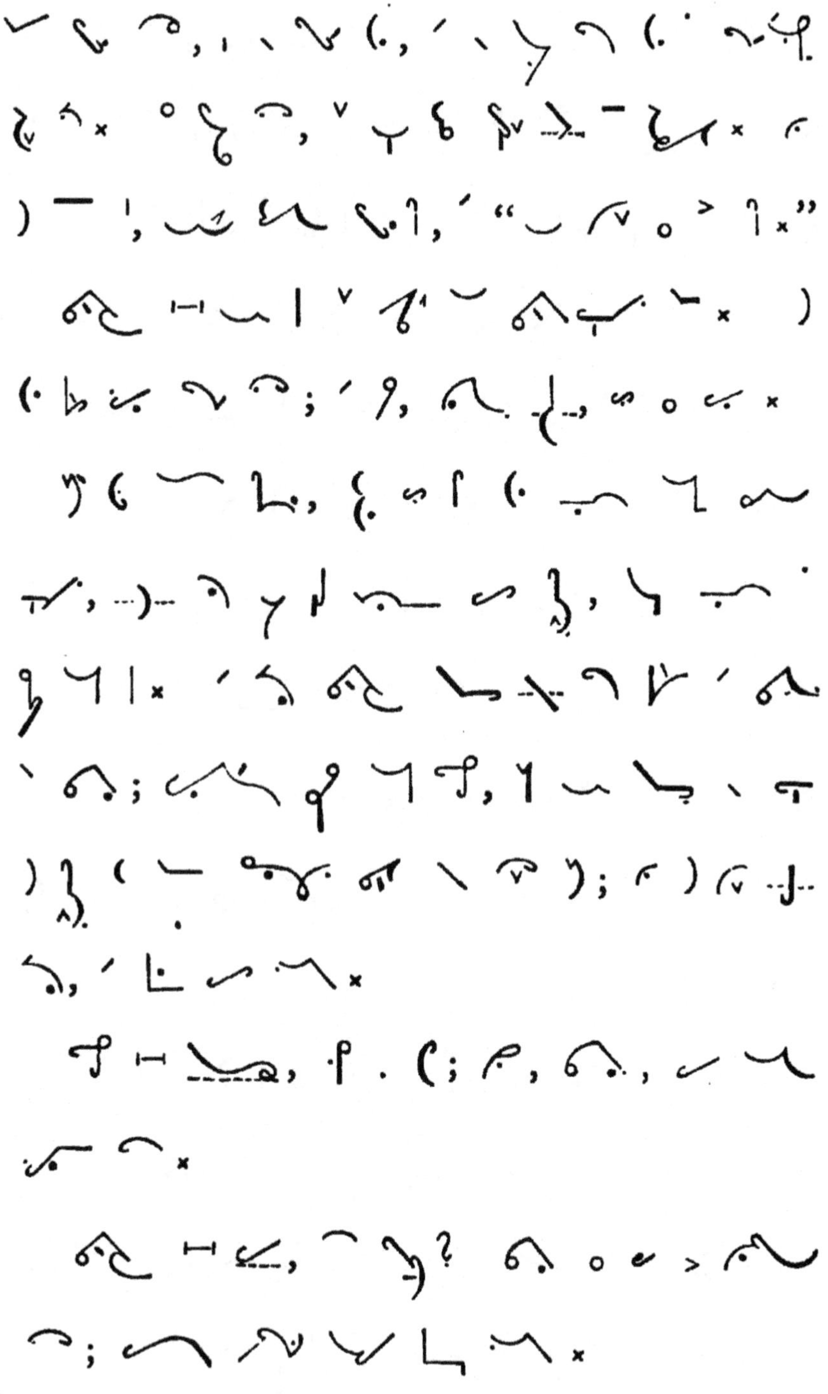

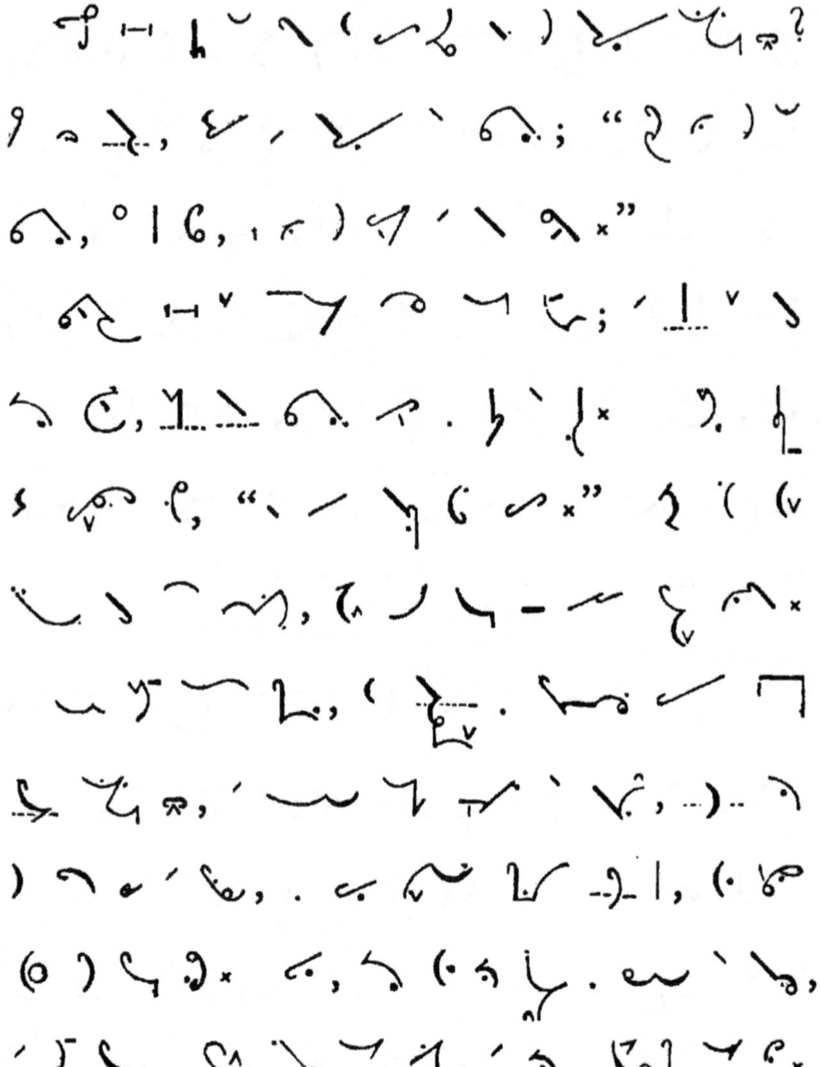

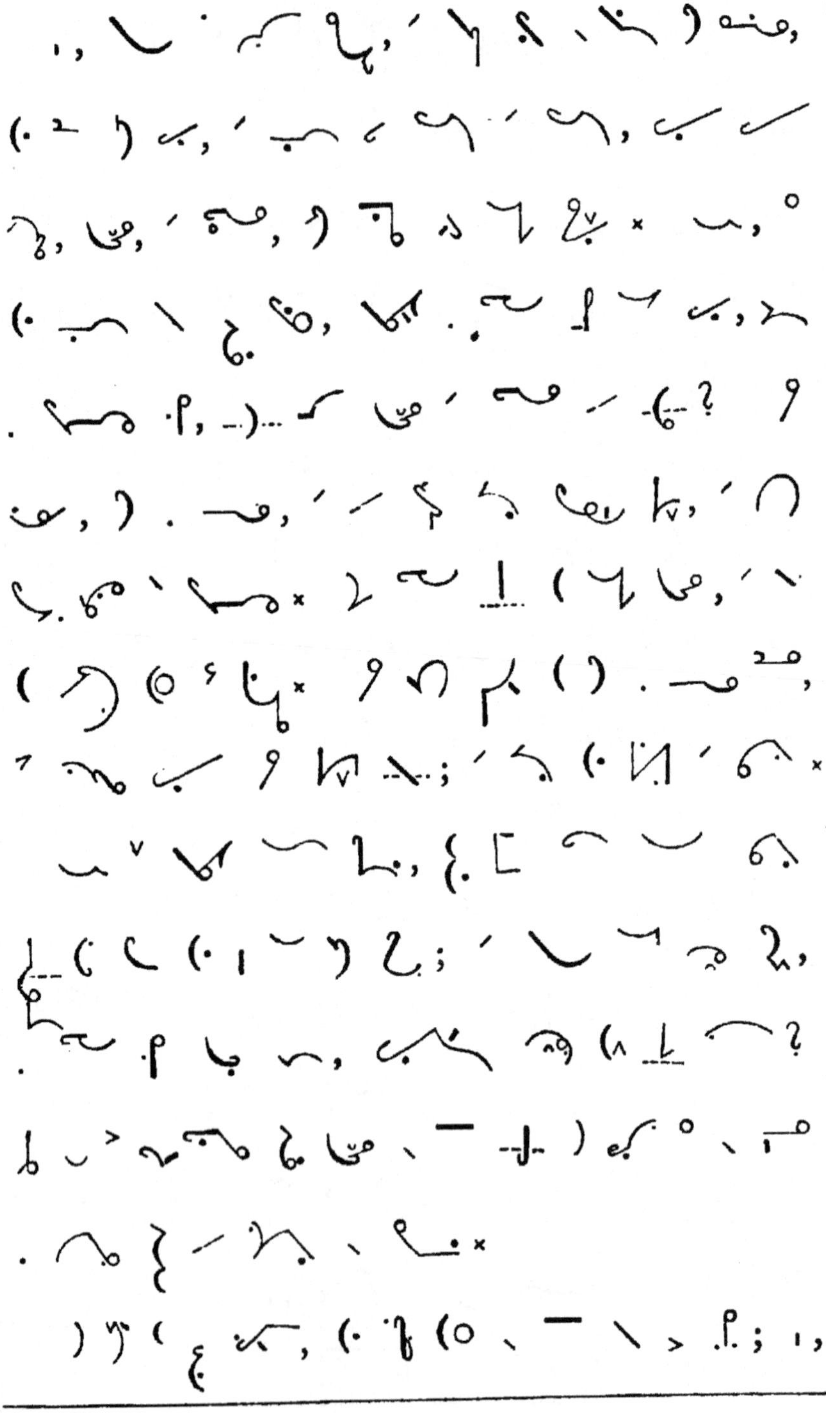

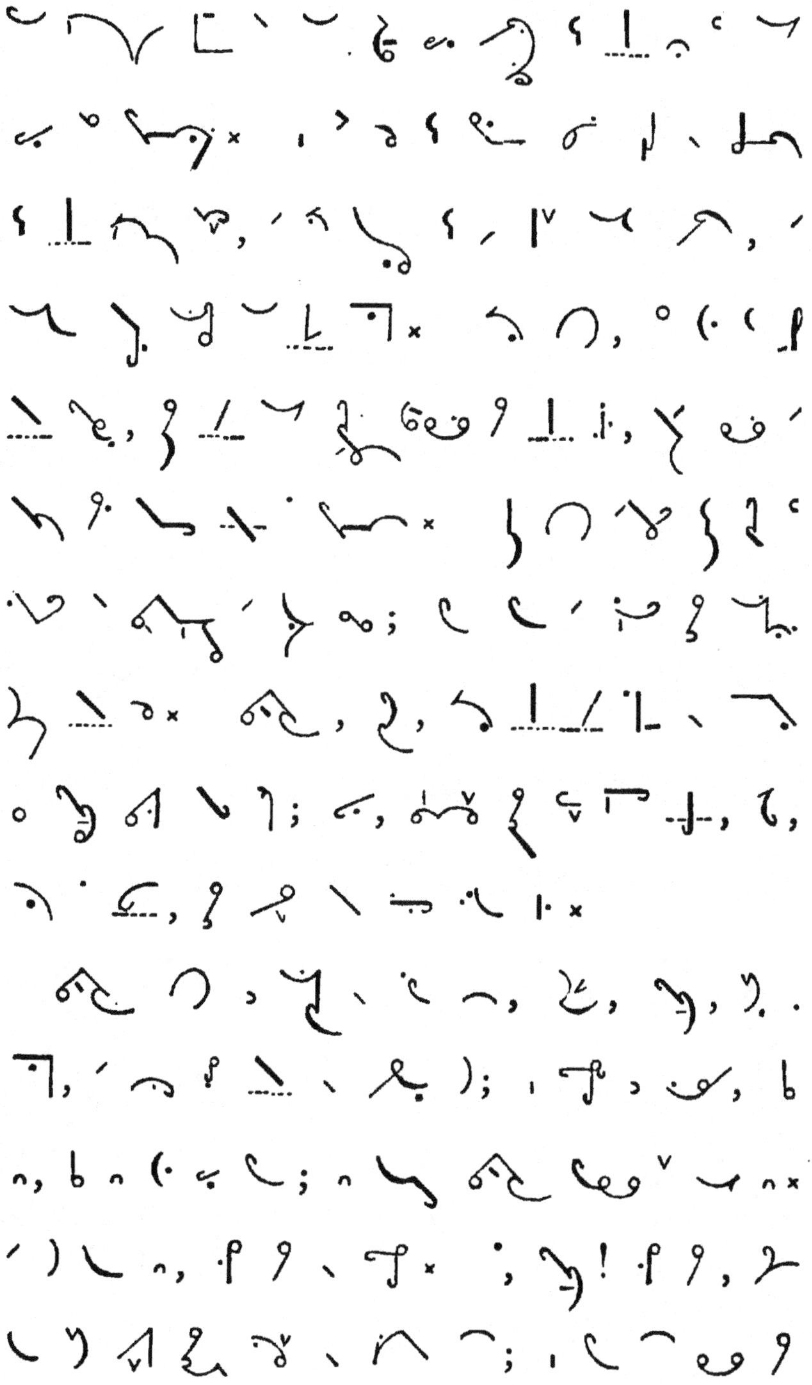

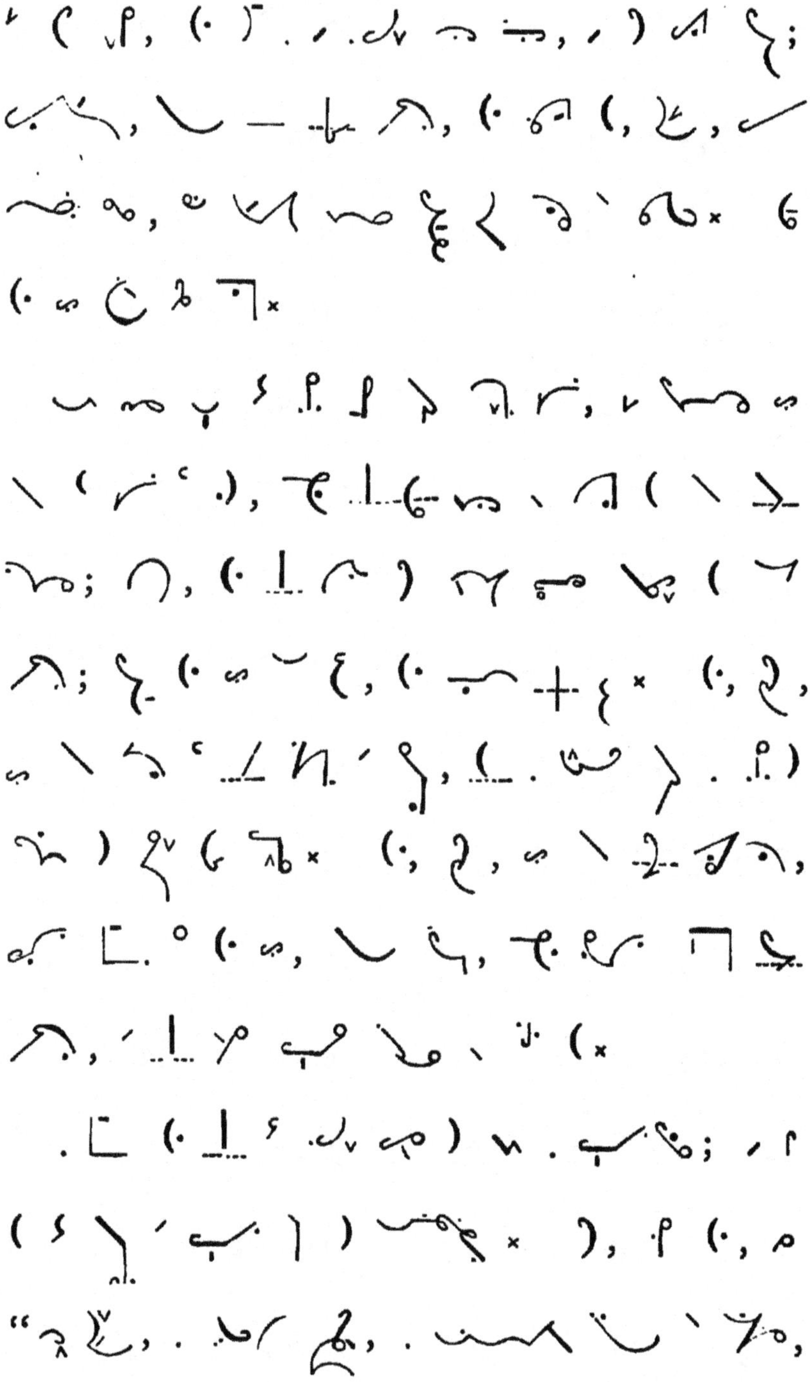

The Narrative Of The Pilgrim's Progress From This World To That Which Is To Come... - Primary Source Edition

John Bunyan